My Least Favorite Team is my Favorite Team

How the Minnesota Vikings have made
me hate every team in professional football

Keith Richotte Jr.

ISBN 10: 1-934248-52-5
ISBN 13: 978-1-934248-52-2

Introduction

This is a story with many beginnings.

The most recent beginning occurred some anonymous night not long ago at maybe midnight...or maybe later...I never did bother to check the time.

The most recent beginning occurred on yet another night I found myself having trouble getting to sleep. It is a common personal affliction and one with which I have, more or less, learned to cope. However, as anyone who has ever found her- or himself in the same situation could attest, such an affliction has one particularly distinct symptom: when you cannot get to sleep, your mind begins to wander.

On this particular anonymous night not long ago my mind was bouncing around the murky waters of my deep psyche like a frog from lily pad to lily pad when it stopped upon an area of an unfortunate level of concern: Vikings. More specifically, the Minnesota Vikings. Even more specifically, the stupid Minnesota Vikings.

For whatever reason, my mind decided to rest upon the topic of my favorite football team. Admittedly, ending one paragraph by claiming that the Vikings are "stupid" and beginning the immediately following paragraph by labeling them as my favorite team would seem, at best, contradictory–perhaps even schizophrenic or purposely self-destructive. Yet, such is the life of a Vikings fan. And while deliberating upon the lads in purple, I came to a startling hypothesis: Was it possible that I could specifically remember a particular slight every other NFL team had perpetrated upon the Vikings in my years of watching them? Was it possible that the Minnesota Vikings had made me hate every other team in the league?

I tossed and turned to find a more comfortable position. Yet, in doing so, I became more uncomfortable with my assertion. After all, there were thirty-one other NFL franchises. That would be, perhaps understatedly, a lot of hate. Oh sure, there were the obvious ones: the Packers, the Bears, the Cowboys. But who in their right mind does not hate those teams? What about some of the others? I mean, did I really hate the Chargers that much?

Then, as I am wont to do in those situations, I began thinking about it a little more deeply. And I realized that I could dredge up some hate for the San Diego Chargers. It seemed impossible on first glance. After all, San Diego is half a continent away geographically, and perhaps even further away culturally, from Minnesota. The Chargers were never one of the teams that busied themselves with trouncing the Vikings in a Super Bowl. In fact, the Chargers managed getting themselves nearly kicked out of the league with their putrid performance in their lone Super Bowl performance against the San Francisco 49ers. Or, at least the powers that were at the time should have seriously considered kicking them out of the sport.

It was the mid-90s. Grunge and the NFC ruled the world. And the collection of ugly cousins that the AFC had been parading to the big game was disgusting enough that even the most devoted of wingmen would have come up with any lame excuse to leave the party early. In fact, the wingman always seemed to leave round about the middle of the second quarter in those days, and you were left knowing that you had another two and a half to three hours of feigning interest and knowing full well that there was no hope for any excitement for the rest of the night.

Nonetheless, despite their relative anonymity and their lack of a direct link to one of those soul-crushing moments that litter Vikings lore like dandelions in an open, unkempt field, I did find that I did have some hate for the Chargers. How is it, might you ask, that I hate the Chargers? Well, good reader, you will have to read on to find out. However, with the Chargers now securely entrenched in the "hate" category, I began making inquiries about other teams that would seem unlikely to engender any real distain, much less hate. The Jets? The Jaguars? What about the Texans?

Clearly, I thought as I tossed and turned once again, that it was not even worth cataloging the NFC teams. As a man in my early thirties, I can honestly tell you that I have been watching the Vikings play football on fall Sundays for at least a quarter of a century. Thusly, I can also honestly tell you that I have seen every NFC team defeat the Vikings at some point or another. Every stinking team. Even the perpetually terrible Arizona Cardinals. In fact, if you are one of those lucky souls who has escaped the wretched existence of life as a Vikings fan, and you happen to know one of my unfortunate brethren, ask this person about the Cardinals. If this person is an actual fan of the team and has been so since at least 2003, I can promise you that she or he will, quite animatedly, tell you about a particular loss to the perpetually terrible Arizona Cardinals. In fact, if you happen to know an actual Green Bay Packers fan (and may whatever divine power that exists out there help you if you do) who has been so since at least 2003, ask her or him about that particular loss. I hate the Cardinals and I hate the NFC.

By the time that I decided not to bother with the NFC, however, Sleep was finally willing to consent to a dance. Much like the person sitting alone at the end of the bar, Sleep looks better and better as the night wears on. Thus, I decided not to pass up the opportunity for which I had much longed. But as Sleep and I joined hands and began our waltz, I vowed that I would renew the project in the morning when I had a clear head and a fresh perspective.

The next day I sat down, determined to resume my inquiry from the previous night: have the Minnesota Vikings made me hate every team in professional football? You hold the answer in your hands.

But that is only one beginning.

This is a story with many beginnings. Another recent beginning occurred in late October of 2006. The Vikings were 4-2 and were starting to get noticed by the talking heads who wonk off about the sport for a living. Yet, even that record did not seem to reflect the positive direction in which the team was headed. There was a relatively new owner, a completely new coach, and there also appeared to be a new attitude. The two notches in the "L" column even seemed somewhat excusable. The Vikings had lost a particularly close game in week three against the Chicago Bears due to of one of the handful of decent plays made by Rex Grossman during that season. Had Rex played the way he would play in the second matchup between the two teams in 2006, undoubtedly the Vikings would have won and would have been leading the division. I hate the Bears. The second blemish was to a plucky, yet seemingly overmatched Bills team. At the time I would have told you that the Vikings had more talent than the Bills that season and that it was "just one of those weeks" that every NFL team must suffer. In retrospect, however, one has to question the plausibility of such an assessment, especially since the back-to-back Bears and Bills games were about the time that it was starting to become apparent that a 38-year-old Brad Johnson had long since given his best to the league and was no longer a functioning NFL quarterback. I hate the Bears and I hate the Bills.

Nonetheless, the Vikings were looking good and were hosting a big, Monday night showdown against the New England Patriots. I distinctly remember thinking and telling others that I honestly believed that the game, against a team that was by the mid-00s constantly flirting with the "dynasty" tag, would be a good barometer for just where the Vikings stood among the class of the NFL. I was correct in that assessment. I also distinctly remember thinking and telling others that, regardless of who was to win, it was going to be a close game. I was incorrect in that assessment. The Patriots, who have diabolically and unceasingly exploited preferable matchups in the Belichick era, more or less abandoned a somewhat suspect running game. Knowing full well that the Vikings were among the better run defenders and among the weaker pass defenders that year, Tom Brady and the Patriots methodically carved up the soft Vikings underbelly and walked up and down the field as if it were a summer afternoon traipse around the Boston Common. The final score of 31-7 was an accurate indicator of just how thoroughly the Vikings had been out-coached and out-played. I hate the Patriots.

That final score was to also be an accurate indicator as to how the season would end. It was the first of a four game slide that would kill a season that could not even be resuscitated with a bizarre victory against the Arizona Cardinals. Yet another Vikings campaign was to fall short. Yet another Vikings season was to end in defeat. Just like every other season that I have watched them. Just like every season that they have ever played.

So characterizes life with this team. The only sure things in this world are death, taxes, and the Vikings finding a way to disappoint a somewhat wavering fan base. (Admit it, Vikings fans. There are too many of us who are rightfully labeled "fair-weather.") I have watched Vikings teams come oh so close. I have watched Vikings teams go down in flames. I have watched Vikings teams that I wished would have gone down in flames. I have paid actual United States currency to a disgustingly cheap, read-haired man for the "privilege" of watching a jarhead with a pencil behind his ear stumble his way through half of a decade in a job for which he was decidedly overmatched. I hate the Randy Ratio. It all ends the same. There are no banners. There are no rings. There is only the empty promise of another season that begins in eight months. Ladies and Gentlemen, your Minnesota Vikings!

Yet, that Monday night loss to the Patriots was only still

another beginning in a story that has many beginnings. This story also began with a countless number of episodes during Mike Tice's faux-reign as the so-called leader of his collection of miscreants. This story began on an excessively cold winter day in January of 1999. This story began when a coach threatened to sue the ownership of the team if the ownership group did not sell the team to the coach. This story began during approximately forty-five playoff losses during the Jerry Burns era. This story began when Darrin Nelson dropped a pass in early 1988. Were I truly vain enough to believe that the heaps of misery that the Vikings dole out on an annual basis were directed only at me, I would tell you that the true beginning to this story occurred about twenty-five years ago when my father let his young son sit on his lap and watch the game with him. But I am not that vain. I know that the real beginning to this story occurred long before I began watching football. It began before I was even born. It began in Super Bowls that were played before I ever knew the bittersweet taste of life. It began with a victory over the Bears in the first-ever game played in franchise history. It began some forty-plus years ago when the scoundrels actually became an NFL franchise. Perhaps it began even long before that, when fools began paying for the opportunity to watch professional athletes ply their trade.

Before we continue the path that is the madness of being a fan of the Minnesota Vikings, I want to take some time to explain myself. I do not have a room in my home painted purple and gold that is devoted to the Vikings. I do not own scads of team paraphernalia, nor is anything that I do own autographed by a member of the team. I do not have a son named Bud nor a daughter named Grant. I have not produced this text (which, I am forced to admit, does resemble a manifesto) in some shack in Montana. I have never been arrested, been accused of stalking, purposely started any bar fights, or taken candy from a baby. I suffer from no diagnosed physical or mental illness, nor can I boast to any of the more common addictions upon which society looks down.

In fact, I am a highly educated man. By the time you read

this, I will have my PhD, a law degree, and an advanced law degree that is so obscure that even most lawyers do not know about it. I do not relate this to you to make any claim to authority. Nor do I arrogantly suggest that eruditeness separates the wheat from the chaff.

Rather, I relate this to you for two reasons. The first is to tell you that the Minnesota Vikings can happen to anyone–even someone who should know better. My somewhat lame excuse is that I really did not have a choice. I was turned into a Vikings fan long before I knew the consequences and I cannot help myself now. Boyhood passions can often grow as big and strong as boys themselves. Yet, ultimately, such an argument does not hold water. If human beings can divest themselves from truly addictive forces, such as alcohol, heroin, and cocaine, then I should be able to keep myself from watching a particular football team every fall Sunday. Clearly I have the capacity to learn, to which the gaudy amount of initials that follow my name would attest. Such moments of self-reflection cause a person to wonder. If the definition of madness is to repeat the same activity over and over again, yet expect different results, and I keep watching the Vikings every fall Sunday year after year, well then...

The second reason I relate this to you is because, after that fateful night that I could not get to sleep, I realized that I did have a problem. Even sleep-deprived and desperately hoping to uncloud my mind, I could still recall a disgusting amount of insult against the Vikings. Although not always immediately obvious (yet sometimes easily springing to mind...I hate the Bears), I eventually was able to find a reason to hate every team in the NFL. That is, again understatedly, a lot of hate. In fact, it is a dangerous amount of hate.

I have long acknowledged that the Vikings were capable of affecting my mood. The outcome of any particular game might mean the difference between a cheerful greeting and smile for the bus driver on Monday morning or an angry torrent of words best left to sailors and late night cable television directed toward the jerk who just cut me off because I had to take my car because I was running late because I did not want to get out of bed Monday morning because the

Vikings lost the previous day.

Yet, this was much more than a foggy grumpiness that would eventually dissipate as the day's temperature warmed. This was hate. Hate wrapped up in thirty-plus different packages. Was this much hate affecting me on a different, much deeper level? How could it not? Was I a worse person because of the Minnesota Vikings? Did I have less patience with my fellow humans? Was I too angry to most fully appreciate the preciously short amount of time we are each given on this earth?

In my personal hierarchy of sports, football sits below hockey and above baseball and basketball. Regardless, it is the Vikings who have, over the years, become my favorite team. And through an unholy mixture of the team's buffoonery, idiocy, and hideous decision-making and playmaking, coupled with the sometimes brilliant, sometimes merely competent efforts of other franchises, the Minnesota Vikings have made me hate every other team in the NFL.

Have you ever watched one of those daytime talk shows? You know the ones–they make it their business to be as self-righteous as possible. Generally, there is some NASCAR fan pushing 400 bills and practicing questionable dental habits on stage. The audience is a collection of judgmental, clucking hens and the host is pretending to be above the fray, all the while provoking the hens as if she or he was shaking the coop. At first, the NASCAR fan is defiant. At first the NASCAR fan will stand up to the hens and the host and proudly proclaim that it is okay to smoke crack or sleep with soft-headed goats or run moonshine through a basement casino. Eventually, however, the resolve of the NASCAR fan is worn down by all of the clucking and caterwauling. Eventually, the NASCAR fan will tearfully, painfully, ashamedly, finally admit that she or he has a problem. And once the admission has been made, all is temporarily resolved.

You know what the problem is with each and every one of those shows? Besides the fact that they provide an avenue for mocking others, thus negating any desire or necessity one might feel for any personal self-reflection or self-improvement? On each and every one of those shows the viewer is told over and over again that admitting you have a problem is the first step. Yet, the pseudo-psychology that dominates these shameless arbiters of societal norms never extends beyond that which is necessary to fill the spaces between commercials. All one ever learns on these faux-educational calamities is that there is a first step and admitting that you have a problem is that magical first step.

Not once, not even once in the entire history of the most destructively useless genre in the history of television has anybody on one of those moronic programs ever thought about, let alone bothered to mention, what the second step might be. And heaven forbid a third or fourth or further steps. Instead, the NASCAR fan, the clucking hens, and the smug host are perfectly content to allow their puerile victory die upon whichever slender vine it was growing. These shows, which negate the possibility of self-reflection for its viewers, also refuse to demand further accountability from those who have finally admitted they have a problem. And thus, we are all happier for not having to grow or explore beyond the comfortable bounds of the forty-four minutes devoted to a program in a television hour.

As such, those who seek the possibility of a second step are often forced to venture out on their own. I was forced to admit that night I could not get to sleep that I have a problem because I watch the Minnesota Vikings. Yet, I have not known what to do about it. There is no group therapy for sports fans. There is only sports talk radio. And that just makes you dumber and angrier. Nonetheless, after that night I could not get to sleep, I realized that I had to do something about all of the hate that the Vikings had made me carry around all of these years. So, I invented a second step.

I wrote this book.

Maybe it will help. Maybe it will not help. But I had to try. Over a quarter century of hate was clogging my arteries. Each continuing indignity was another purple platelet getting stuck in my veins. I might have been another Mike Tice–coached game away from a heart attack. I might still yet be one hideous interception away from a stroke. I need to get rid of this hate so that I can finally have a chance at a normal life where the exploits of men like Tommy Kramer, DJ Dozier, and Jeff Brady have no effect on me. Please help me by sharing the pain that the Vikings have caused. Please read why I hate each and every team in the NFL.

Let us begin.

Part I – The AFC

As was already noted, that fateful, restless night when the hypothesis of hate came to me I knew full well that it was pointless to bother analyzing the teams of the NFC. Those teams were a given. I hated them.

The real challenge to the hypothesis, I understood rather quickly, would be the AFC. Undoubtedly, the conference could produce some readily hateable candidates, most specifically each of the four teams that shellacked the Vikings in their four Super Bowl appearances.

Yet, the very nature of the NFL schedule is such that it would have seemed to make my hypothesis a virtual impossibility. After all, even though I had logged over a quarter of a century watching the Vikings tangle with various opponents, I had still only seen the Purple do battle with some of these teams a mere handful of times. Some even less.

Thus, the real quandary that night I spent tossing and turning was whether I could honestly say that I really had some hate for EVERY team in the AFC. My first thought, after recognizing this potentially devastating stumbling block to my theory about the all-encompassing hate that the Vikings have produced, was that maybe I did not even have enough hate for half of the teams in the conference.

Then I thought about it some more. And the more I thought about it, the more it became clear that I had more hate for the AFC than I realized. I remembered certain games and certain plays and other various activities by AFC franchises that came bubbling to the surface of my consciousness with an ease that was a bit troubling.

Nonetheless, the question remained. Despite the effervescence my AFC hate had, the Vikings played these teams with an irregularity that would seem to preclude the possibility of any real passion. It is familiarity, the old adage stipulates, that breeds contempt. And in the hierarchy of familiarity, most of these AFC teams could only be, at best, understood as acquaintances. So, the question remained, do I really hate every team in the AFC?

It turns out that I do. Here is why.

AFC West

Denver Broncos

Four Super Bowl losses. Uniforms that seem, to the maladjusted and uninspired, to be hideously ugly. A home field advantage that starts ferociously and only grows as the snow flies. An all-time great at quarterback who could make as many plays with his legs as with his arm.

Here we have a concise, accurate description of the Denver Broncos and the history of the franchise, do we not? Four simple sentences that convey a reasonably full sense of Broncos football, most particularly in the pre–Terrell Davis era. Admittedly, the opening paragraph neglects to mention the two Super Bowl championships. But there is a reason for this omission that will be explained in due time.

Regardless, let us return our attention to how the opening paragraph conveys a sense of this franchise. Who could forget the orange jerseys and the orange helmets emblazoned with a horse seemingly desperately trying to escape from a gigantic letter D? Even though the team has long since abandoned those outfits, the new uniforms have also received a less-than-favorable reception amongst the sports public.

Nonetheless, whatever uniforms the team has been sporting, it has managed to win quite a few games in Mile High Stadium (there will be no corporate names of any stadium in the project. Period.) The snow and the elevation have made Denver a tough place to play from the beginning of the team's inception. It is a true and distinct home field advantage.

Unfortunately for the franchise, there has yet to be a Super Bowl played in the Mile High City, when the Broncos could have most used a home field advantage. After all, who could forget those four Super Bowl losses? Each of which produced decidedly uncompetitive contests.

In the last three of those losses, the team was lead by the aforementioned all-time great quarterback: John Elway. Upon his retirement, Elway was favorably compared to the best of those who have ever played the position. He was one of the elites with the stats to prove it. Unquestionably in the top five, if not the greatest quarterback to ever strap on a helmet and cleats.

So there you have it, an opening paragraph that succinctly describes the Denver Bronco franchise, most particularly before their two Super Bowl victories. So what about this brief detailing could a Minnesota Vikings fan find to be offensive? How could a seemingly innocent description of the history of one of the most distinct NFL franchises raise a Vikings fan's ire?

Because the Denver Broncos stole that opening paragraph. And then they changed it.

There was a period, long before the professional exploits of John Elway and his heap of last-minute comebacks, when that opening paragraph would have perfectly described the history of the Minnesota Vikings. The Vikings, after all, were the first team to lose a fourth Super Bowl (or a second or a third for that matter). Not to mention there are no shortage of faux-fashion mavens willing to decry the team's uniforms (particularly with the recent additions of the wholly unnecessary side piping). And long before a Teflon dome separated the Vikings from the harsh seasonal elements (and consequently provided Packers fans with a convenient reason to self-righteously proclaim that they are more dedicated to their team because they drunkenly invite frostbite on their Sunday afternoons at the stadium), Minnesota was a harrowing road trip for opposing foes. Finally, the Vikings had an all-time great at quarterback: Fran Tarkenton. He was a scrambler who ultimately built a mighty impressive career for himself. While most known for the plays he made with his legs, Tarkenton retired as the NFL's all-time leader in passing yards and touchdowns.

But then came John Elway. While Elway cannot be blamed for the first of the Broncos' Super Bowl losses, he played an integral part of the next three. And when they were trounced by San Francisco for that magical fourth loss (with Elway making a less-than-Namath-like guarantee of "We'll show up"), the Denver Broncos became the Minnesota Vikings. They stole the thunder.

Whereas Minnesota formerly could at least claim its measure of sports ignominy, after Super Bowl XXIV they were no longer alone. In fact, they had been replaced. The Broncos became the butt of all the jokes. Denver became the symbol of futility and just not being quite good enough. Their claim to this reputation was so strong that they were even lampooned on The Simpsons. So tight was the Bronco stranglehold on their pop-culture identity that people actually began forgetting that the Vikings were the first team to lose four Super Bowls (or two or three, for that matter). People honestly forgot that the Vikings franchise and fans had been living with the four-loss yoke around their necks for much, much longer. The Vikings, it seemed, even lost out on the losing.

Then it all changed again. As Elway was nearing the end of a distinguished, yet somewhat incomplete career, the Broncos found a dominant rusher in Terrell Davis and enough competent pieces on defense to make their march to two titles. I was actually reasonably pleased when they won their first Super Bowl. First and foremost, they beat the Packers. Had I been forced to watch Brett Favre and Reggie White hoist another Lombardi Trophy, it would have been akin to being forced to watch someone punch my mother in the face for a second consecutive year. Secondly, I figured that, since Denver had finally shed the loser label, the Vikings would again reclaim their rightful place as the NFL's greatest tough luck loser (the exploits of the Buffalo Bills notwithstanding).

The second Bronco Super Bowl victory was much more difficult to swallow for a couple of reasons. First, they crushed a seriously overmatched Atlanta Falcons team. While I do not begrudge the Broncos for beating the team that they are scheduled to play, any true Vikings fan knows they should not have been matched up against the Falcons that year. The Vikings are the team the Broncos should have been playing in Super Bowl XXXIII. The hows and whys of the situation with Atlanta will be discussed in a later section. What is important to note here is that had Denver matched up with the Vikings, one has to believe that the football gods would have found a way to let the Vikings win. After all, it would have been too cruel for the Broncos, who the previous year had finally been released from their four-Super-Bowl-loss torment, to hang a fifth Super Bowl loss on the franchise that they had replaced as the symbol of NFL futility. Even the football gods, malicious as they can be, are not that heartless.

Second, after they beat the Falcons, the Broncos became one of the small pantheons of "model franchises." The rest of the league looked to the Broncos as the guide for winning football and how to properly run an organization. In two short years, the Broncos went from a laughingstock to the top of the NFL world.

The Broncos proved that it could happen. Losing a fourth Super Bowl was bad, but it did not have to be the end of the world for a franchise. It was possible to win. Losing a fourth Super Bowl did not make a team "unlucky" or "ill fated" or put that team in any other state in which they were unable to control their own destiny. The

Broncos, and their eventual success, forced Vikings fans to realize that the Vikings' inability to win the big one was the team's own fault. The Broncos opened our eyes. And what we were forced to see was that our favorite franchise has generally been run by idiots and clowns who have routinely destroyed the possibility for success and for that elusive Super Bowl victory. It was our moment of clarity.

I hate the Denver Broncos.

AFC WEST

Kansas City Chiefs

We shall set aside, for the moment, the nickname of this franchise. We shall set aside the fact that I married into a family that has actively protested an unconscionably insensitive portrayal of an entire race of peoples. We shall set aside that drunken louts dress and behave, on the one day of the week that most of them presumably consider the most sacred, in a manner that deliberately and perhaps even maliciously parodies the culture, heritage, lifestyle, and religious beliefs of the first Americans. We shall set a more thorough discussion of these issues aside for another section and another team (exactly which team should be easy to figure out).

Racist nickname and behavior of the fans aside (for the time being), there are other reasons to hate the Kansas City Chiefs. Most of them have to do with a game that was played about a half a decade before I was born.

As a man in his early thirties, I have to confess that I have not as fully suffered as the generation of Vikings fans that preceded me. I was not able to experience any of the Super Bowl losses as they were happening. In fact, I was only alive for one of them, and was much too young to be consciously aware of the defeat. So, my understandings of the Super Bowl losses have come from my Viking fan forbearers and from old films about the games.

These conditions might suggest to the feeble-minded, cognitively impaired pundits that routinely populate sports talk radio and FOX News that I have not truly suffered as a Vikings fan. Convincing those imbeciles otherwise would take, at minimum, a humorous yet true-to-life, book-length account of the team's grievous errors and mishaps affected upon its fan base (Hmm...).

But I have suffered. Kansas City, of course, defeated the Minnesota Vikings in Super Bowl IV. It was the first of the four losses. And while I was not yet alive on that January day of 1970 when the game was played, I have lived through that Super Bowl loss as much as any Vikings fan. And the reason why I have lived through that Super Bowl loss as much as any Vikings fan is due to the most addictive substance ever created: NFL Films.

If the Minnesota Vikings are my cocaine then NFL Films are my crack. They are cheaper, they are more readily available, and they are as nearly impossible to quit. I simply cannot help myself. Whenever I stumble upon some showing of whatever they happen to be playing on television, I stop my life in that precise moment and watch until it is completely finished. It does not matter whether it is as serious as something like a "Greatest Quarterbacks to Ever Play the Game" program or as silly as a "Football Follies" episode or as irrelevant as "The 1983 Tampa Bay Buccaneers: Aiming Upward From the Cellar" retrospective. I will watch.

Like all addictions, my inability to remove myself from NFL Films programming has some nasty side effects. The most debilitating of those side effects is that I have watched every Vikings Super Bowl loss in five-minute, half-hour, and hour-long versions several times. Each NFL Films production of a Vikings' Super Bowl loss is painful in its own right. Each finds its own way to suck with a unique flair. However, the Kansas City loss is particularly galling for one reason:

Hank Stram.

For those not in the know, Hank Stram was, inarguably, the most successful head coach in Kansas City's history. He was the head coach of the team during that Super Bowl season and a reasonably poor announcer for some time thereafter. Yet, for as annoying as he could be during his color commentary days, he was at least tenfold worse in those NFL Films packages of Super Bowl IV.

It was bad enough that the people at NFL Films involved in the production of this particular episode lauded Stram as if he was a hero from antiquity whose game plan for the Super Bowl had been delivered directly from the gods atop Mount Olympus. Stram cannot be faulted for the decisions made by the Sabol cabal. What Stram can be faulted for, however, is his own ridiculous commentary during the game.

During the course of the NFL Films coverage of Super Bowl IV, a disturbing and inordinate amount of time is spent watching and listening to Stram on the sideline. Stram, for his part, plays the role of a happy-go-lucky character through his folksy sayings and allegedly delightful noises. At one point, Stram actually implores his team to "matriculate" the ball down the field. Nobody, absolutely nobody, in all of humankind within the last seventy-five years has used the word matriculate without a sense of irony, humor, or in a sophomoric attempt to turn it into a euphemism for sex. Except Hank Stram.

This is hardly the most egregious example of this absurdity, however. Throughout the course of Stram's Super Bowl sound bites, we quickly and repeatedly learn that his favorite play is sixty-five-toss-power-trap. By unofficial count, the words "sixty-five-toss-power-trap" come out of the mouth of Hand Stram 29,647 times during the NFL Films production. It keeps wearing on you until it slowly grinds you into madness. Sixty-five-toss-power-trap. Sixty-five-toss-power-trap. SIXTY-FIVE-TOSS-POWER-TRAP!

And if it is not actual words, then it is the sounds. Stram is chock full of giggles and blatherings and excited utterances that pepper his dialogue. It is a disturbing array of noises that suggest that there is a small gnome that lives within Stram's pants and is constantly tickling him with a feather. The whole presentation comes across in such a down-home, aw-schucks, golly-gee manner that one is forced to wonder what sort of dark secrets are lurking beneath the surface of all of that folksiness. It is painful to watch. Particularly because it is impossible to doubt that Stram's counterpart that day, Bud Grant, was wholly incapable of providing similar fodder for such tripe. Had the Vikings been victorious that day, the words "sixty-five-toss-power-trap" would not currently be slowly yet methodically chipping away at my sanity.

I hate the Kansas City Chiefs.

AFC WEST

Oakland Raiders

The obvious reason for a Vikings fan to hate the Raiders is, of course, Super Bowl XI. It was to be the last of the four Super Bowl losses and the only one for which I was alive (although too young to remember). Like with Kansas City (and with Miami and Pittsburgh), I lived through this uncompetitive Super Bowl loss through NFL Films–the lasting impression being a close-up, slow motion shot of Willie Brown determinedly breathing through his mouth as he housed a seventy-five yard interception. Brown's mustachioed, mouth-breathing look of determination was almost as intimidating and ugly as the game's final score.

I do hate the Raiders for that Super Bowl loss. However, I probably do not hate them for that Super Bowl loss as much as I should. I really hate for them for a different reason. I hate them because, long before I had a more firm grasp on the Vikings' losing lore, the Raiders were my "second team" for a long time. And then they got stupid. And then former Vikings went to play for them.

Let us start with the concept of a "second team," which should be pretty self-explanatory. Nonetheless, the idea requires further elaboration because the increasing fear and paranoia that envelopes the world in which we live has made the second team more and more rare. A fan may have one team that is, far and away, her or his favorite. That team is her or his "first team." Yet, a fan may also find herself or himself rooting for another club in the same league, and she or he may do so for a variety of reasons. Perhaps that other club employs a player from a local college, or maybe the other team has a particularly exciting style of play, or maybe they just have cool uniforms. Whether the rationale is meaningful or frivolous, our hypothetical fan likes another team other than her or his primary one. That is that fan's second team.

Were it just a matter of my wanting to confess to you that the Raiders, during the Marcus Allen and Bo Jackson years, were my second team, I would not have wasted my time writing this section. After all, why should you care that I desperately needed the Raiders to beat Washington in Super Bowl XVIII (for deeply personal reasons that I have no intention revealing in this project)? Instead, I have confessed to having a second team because such an admission has truly become a confession. I am revealing that the Raiders were my second team for a number of years because I believe in the right to have a second team.

We are living in a world that is proffering more and more rules by which to live, particularly for men. Every time you flip on a television or turn on the radio or walk past a newsstand, you are inundated with somebody spouting off about the "new rules for men" or "men laws." This silly trend, which seems to have exacerbated in the last ten years or so, belies a growing fear about masculinity and the roles of men within society. Whether the men of the world are actually feeling this fear, I do not presume to know. What I do know, however, is that those who shape culture want the men of the world to respond to this fear.

The provocation to respond to this fear is found nearly everywhere. Sometimes it is played for laughs (with varying degrees of success) by men like Jim Belushi and Kevin James whose television characters act like "men," but who are routinely browbeaten by fictional television wives who are one-third their size. Most often, however, this fear is meant to shape behavior. Often, one will turn on the television to find a well-chiseled chap telling you that real men use the lotion found in the gray, square bottle to smooth their face after a shave. And if it is not aftershave, then you are told that a real man drives this truck or drinks this beer or uses this soap. We are constantly given rules by which to live. This is a clear indication of fear. Whenever an entity has too many rules, whether it be a country or a corporation or even a gender, it is a reflection of that entity's uncertainty with itself.

What does this have to do with a second team? The ever-growing amount of laughably absurd rules has worked its way into the dominion of sports fandom. As the supposed crisis in masculinity has grown, so too have the number of rules on how to be a proper fan has grown. They apparently teach us all how to root for our teams "like a man." Thus, you have sports talk radio wonks telling you that you cannot like more than one team at once or that the only teams you are allowed to like are the ones in your town or the ones your dad liked. A whole system of "laws" has been created to regulate your behavior as a sports fan.

The rules of being a sports fan, along with the "rules of men" in general, are a steaming pile of freshly dropped horse feces. Presumably some of these rules were crafted to identify the bandwagon jumpers from the true fans. Truth be told, I hate the sniveling, spineless scuzballs who only wear the team apparel of the latest champion as much as the next guy. But these gasbags are easy to recognize amongst the loyalists. We do not need a rigid system of mindless rules to ferret out those losers.

It is these fan laws that have been slowly eroding your right to have a second team. Well, no more, I say. It is okay to have a second team. It is okay to hope another franchise wins a championship if your favorite franchise is not going to win it. What is more, it is perfectly acceptable for your second team to change. If that local college player retires or gets traded, or if there is a coaching change and the style of play is not as fun as it once was, or if they change their uniforms to something hideously ugly, then go ahead and dump your second team. If the die-hards want to sneer at you and call you names, then tell them to take a long walk out of a short airplane. You do not need to live by a stupid set of rules that were created to teach the insecure and unstable how to "be a man."

As I have stated before, the Raiders were once my second team. Now they are not, and they have not been for a good long while. Basically, they ceased to be interesting after Bo Jackson got injured (on a play that, to this day, does not look like it could have possibly caused as much damage as it did). They were no longer on television as much and it was not worth the time and trouble to keep up with them (these were the days before the internet was widely available and made it exceptionally easy for students to cheat on their term papers and book reports).

For a good, long time after that the Raiders were among the mass of teams that I did not give much of a rip about. But then a couple of players changed it all. The first was Rich Gannon. Many remember Gannon for his remarkable 2002 season where he seemingly underwent a Kurt Warner–esque resurrection to become the NFL's MVP. Others remember his five-interception performance in the Super Bowl that season. I remember being completely floored by the fact that Gannon was anywhere near a Super Bowl without having to pay for his own ticket or sell popcorn, let alone winning the MVP award.

Gannon began his NFL career with the Vikings. Prior to his breakthrough season, he was, in my memory, one of the major players in two of the lamest quarterback controversies to which I have ever witnessed. The first was in the early '90s or so when a young Gannon was the heir apparent to an increasingly mediocre Wade Wilson. After Gannon won the job, he did little to rally the fans to his cause. A couple of years of uninspired play later, Gannon was forced aside by Sean Salisbury. Wilson, of course, did not do much in the NFL after his stint with the Vikings and Salisbury is now much better known for making a donkey's rear out of himself on ESPN on a regular basis then for his playing career. Gannon seemed destined for a similar fate. Yet, a decade later he was voted as the most valuable player in all of professional football. It just did not seem possible. The Gannon I remembered was the one that played in the Super Bowl, not the one that won all of the accolades. Ultimately, the fact that he could find so much success so many years after being so terrible with the Vikings was supremely annoying.

The other player who changed my perception of the Raiders was, of course, Randy Moss. The often wonderful, often terrible, always explosive journey from Moss's rookie of the year campaign to his eventual trade to the Raiders for a first round pick and a bag of peanuts was an allegorical tale of unfulfilled promise and of one man's desperate inability to be happy and/or satisfied at any point in his life.

Moss's rookie year of 1998 was absolutely magical. More time will be spent on this particularly crushing year in another section. Suffice it to say that the sky was the limit for Moss and for the hopes of Vikings fans. Despite the eventual team disappointment of 1998, Moss continued to put up the kind of stats that projected him to be one of, if not the, greatest of all time.

As is so often the case, however, all of the talent came with a price. Some of Moss's activities were best described as "antics." He made stupid statements, he was caught with pot in his car, he (sort of) ran over a traffic cop, he walked off the field before the game was finished, and so on and so forth. The apologists (myself included) were able to rationalize away most of the behavior. But it became increasingly clear, even to the most blindly loyal Vikings fans, that Randy Moss was the kind of guy who was never going to be happy, no matter how much he got his way or how much the whole world bent over backwards for him. And he was intent on sabotaging whatever situation in which he found himself.

So, he was traded. To the Raiders. All of the promise that

his rookie year produced was finally and totally spent without any Super Bowl championships to show for it. The silver and black number eighteen was, from that moment forward, a symbol of both that promise and its failure. Randy Moss was supposed to lead the Vikings to the promised land. Instead, in the end, he slinked off of a field before a game was done in Washington D.C. and more or less kept walking all the way to the Bay Area, as unhappy as ever. When he left, he claimed to be happy to finally be out of the Vikings' organization. When he was traded from Oakland to New England two years later, he claimed to be hurt that the Vikings traded him away. In that moment, Randy Moss had officially blamed 99.99999% of the people in the world for his misfortune. Perhaps someday soon he will find the real culprit for all of his troubles.

Within twenty years the Oakland Raiders went from my second team to an outpost for Vikings' rejects who neatly sum up the failures, missed opportunities, and squandered potential of the purple and gold.

I hate the Oakland Raiders.

AFC WEST

San Diego Chargers

Have you ever had one of those friends who was just never able to hold on to a good thing? Maybe your friend is almost deliberately self-destructive with her or his good fortune? Have you ever been friends with Randy Moss?

You know the type of person that I am describing. In fact, I am willing to wager that we have all known someone like the hypothetical friend described above. She or he cannot just leave well enough alone.

Is there anything more hopeless than watching that friend throw away the good things that she or he has acquired in her or his life? Maybe that friend has a nice sports car. Maybe the sports car would not have won any drag races that it entered, but it was fun and powerful and made you just a little envious when your friend picked you up. Even so, the friend of yours is not happy. She or he is constantly talking about trading up or getting a new paint job or having some expensive amenity installed. Finally one day, your friend calls you up and wants to show off her or his new car. And when you see it, you want to strangle your friend. She or he traded in her or his sweet, cherry red sports car for some boxy, ugly "luxury" car because it has a few more needless bells and whistles and was made by a manufacturer with a reputation for being expensive.

Even worse, have you ever watched that friend sabotage a perfectly decent relationship with a really wonderful partner for no apparent reason? Maybe your buddy's girlfriend (I am going to adopt a male, heteronormative point of view for the remainder of this paragraph for the purpose of fleshing out this example; please accept my apologies if you are more comfortable with a different point of view) is not perfect in the societally crafted sense of beauty and companionship. And maybe she would not mesh all that well with some other people that you know. However, she is perfect for him and all of his goofy idiosyncrasies. And it is clear that she wants to be with him, even though he is destined to destroy all of the decency and goodness in his life. Despite her devotion and the obviousness of how well they are matched, your buddy still complains all the time about her. Generally the complaints revolve around the stupidest little things. Maybe he thinks that the way that she flosses her teeth is really gross or that he is convinced that her parents are kind of cold to him or maybe her boobs are not big enough. So, he breaks up with her. A decent woman whose lone mistake was giving a darn about an idiot is left with a broken heart and, about a week after they split up, your buddy is now complaining about being single again.

The thing about the San Diego Chargers is that they should not be all that offensive to a Minnesota Vikings fan. And, in one sense, they really are not very offensive at all. I really only have one memory of the Vikings playing the Chargers that jumps to mind readily. In the 2003 season, the Mike Tice–led Vikings jumped out of the chute with six consecutive wins before stumbling their way to a final record of 9-7. During that less-than-magical year, they became only the second team in NFL history to win their first six games and fail to make the playoffs. Four of the team's seven losses that season were utterly inexcusable as they were delivered by the four teams that would tie for the league's worst record.

Take a moment to dwell upon that: in 2003 four teams tied with league-worst 4-12 records. And the Vikings were responsible for one of the four wins for each one of those teams. It was the most inglorious example of playing down to an opponent in NFL history.

San Diego was one of those 4-12 teams in 2003. The contest was Doug Flutie's last shining game as an NFL quarterback. Flutie unmercifully dissected the Vikings in a never-close 42-28 Charger victory. A few weeks of ineffective play later, Flutie would be replaced by Drew Brees and Flutie's unexpectedly long career was finally over.

That is pretty much the only real memory I have of a game between the Vikings and the Chargers. And, I will confess that I am still more angry at the Vikings then I am at the Chargers for that loss. That whole 2003 season was full of gutless performances and squandered opportunities. Blaming the Chargers would be like blaming the dog for running away when it was your crazy, twitchy, incontinent uncle who left the gate to the yard open.

So, I must not hate the Chargers, right? Wrong. Even though I cannot come up with an adequate example of how they have personally wronged the Minnesota Vikings, I still believe that the San Diego Chargers have wronged the entire NFL and all of humanity. I hate the Chargers for being that friend who can never seem to figure out how good she or he had it before she or he ruins it.

I am loathe to accept that Chris Berman and I have anything in common. His tired shtick of showing clips of himself when he was younger, bad puns masquerading as nicknames, and strange noises (which makes me believe that when Hank Stram finished coaching the gnome that lived in his pants picked up and moved on to Berman's prodigious trousers) is enough to make me swear off SportsCenter for a week. Nonetheless, he makes one supremely salient point every football season (and he usually makes it about forty-seven times during the season). The San Diego Chargers used to have the best uniforms in all of football, if not all of sports.

The powder blue of the Chargers' old uniforms stands in

stark contrast to the rest of the uniforms in the NFL and looks awfully sharp on a football field. The white helmets with the lightning bolt and the player's number on the side provide a refreshing splash of individuality, yet not so much that it distracts from the rest of the uniform or from the team as a whole. In their own way, they are just as intimidating as the uniforms of the Raiders or Steelers or Cowboys. I have yet to meet a human being that prefers the monstrosities that they have been wearing ever since they got rid of the powder blue. Yet, the Chargers stubbornly refuse to change them back to what they should be.

It is not very often in this world when you are blessed with something that others envy. Nor is it every day when that which suits you best is something that you can readily have or possess. When you do have it, you would do well to cherish it. However, there are those who cannot recognize these facts and are more than willing to cast aside what is best for them in the hopes of something impossibly better just around the corner. Those people are fools.

I hate the San Diego Chargers.

AFC SOUTH

Houston Texans

Arrogance is bad. Arrogance combined with a serious lack of creativity is much, much worse.

Of all of the teams in the NFL it would seem that the Houston Texans would be the one team least likely to raise a Viking fan's ire. After all, the franchises have only met on the field once in the Texans' short history.

The October 2004 matchup ended much closer than it should have. The Vikings blew a comfortable lead when a shaky defense allowed the Texans to score twenty-one points in the fourth quarter. The game seemed destined for failure when it headed for overtime. The Texans had all of the momentum and showed no signs of slowing. In fact, it looked like it was going to be David Carr's "breakout" game, which would propel him to the upper echelon of NFL quarterbacks. I suspect that Texan fans suffered through at least one or two of these ultimately disappointing types of games each year before Carr was let go after the 2006 season.

Nonetheless, fate was to smile upon the Vikings that day in

Houston. Daunte Culpepper found Marcus Robinson for a fifty-yard touchdown to end it about halfway through overtime. The winning score came shortly after Robinson dropped what would have been another sure touchdown to end the game. In the end, however, all was well that ended well.

That one game, a Vikings victory nonetheless, would seem to add up to very little hate. The Vikings have never lost to the Texans. Ever. The Texans have not been around long enough, or been decent enough during their short existence, to create all that much animosity. They do not immediately spring to mind as poor losers despite all of their experience at it. None of their players seem all that much like villains. They have never employed a coach that was immediately and enjoyably detestable (wherefore art thou, Buddy Ryan?).

So, how could a Vikings fan ever conjure up any actual hate for a team that has left little impression on the NFL during its very short existence? How is this even remotely possible?

Luckily, I hated the Texans long before the team ever took a real snap in an NFL game.

Sports in the United States has grown to the point where it is as bloated and disgusting as those people who are only able to leave their house by removing a wall. And as those unusually large people must realize as they are being lifted out of their bed with the help of a crane, there are serious consequences for letting the situation get out of hand. One of the starkest consequences of the explosion of sports in the United States is that the marketing mentality has gained a greater hold on some of the basic decisions concerning the games that are played.

One point should be made clear before this line of reasoning continues: it would be supremely naïve to think that there was a simpler, gentler time when professional (and collegiate) sports were about just the game and were not concerned about selling tickets and ball caps. As long as there have been professional sports, there have been promotional giveaways and silly contests and other assorted goofy attempts to draw people to the ballparks and arenas. Yet, it seems like in the past those giveaways and contests and other goofiness were created by people who still cared about the sport in which they were involved. In the last twenty years or so, it seems like the attempts to get you to plunk down your hard-earned cash for tickets and jerseys and posters are crafted by soulless suits who could care less about the sport and more about whatever latest trend will separate you from your money.

This

movement, coupled with the expansion of the various sports leagues, has lead to some absurd results. Some teams now change their uniforms every three years or so. Perhaps more disturbingly, with the growth of sports leagues beginning in the late '80s and continuing into the new century, those soulless suits who now make the decisions in sports decided that team nicknames had to be edgy and different. Thus were born the Avalanche and the Heat. Some team nicknames made sense, like the Rockies. However, we had to endure a whole spate of alternate jerseys and colors more appropriate for a fashion runway then an arena. Those Rockies fans who were saved embarrassment with a reasonable nickname were then forced to choose between approximately 492 different combinations of hats and jerseys.

Within this desperate attempt to be corporate America's version of cutting edge, the purpose of the nickname was lost. Nicknames are supposed to evoke the kind of ferocity with which one would like the team to play, such as the Lions, Falcons, and Giants. If not ferocity, then nicknames are supposed to appeal to an aspect of the home city with which the community can identify, such as the 49ers, Packers, and Steelers.

I suppose the Houston Texans can be commended for at least attempting to buck the trend. I suppose by calling their team the "Texans" the good folks in control of the Houston franchise were trying to both evoke ferocity and a connection to the community. So, give them some credit for that.

Nonetheless, when I first heard the name for the NFL's newest team, I wanted to throw up. Texas has always struck me as a supremely arrogant state, and this was one more example of why it was so. Seriously, what is with you, Texas? Just because a bunch of white guys moved onto Mexican (and before that Spanish and before that Indian) land and decided they had formed their own country for a while does not make you unique or special. White folks had been doing that sort of garbage around the world for centuries before there was a Republic of Texas. It really is not that much to be proud of.

That arrogance, coupled with the fact that Texas has a history of stealing and/or abusing Minnesota teams (not to mention that they helped launch the political career of one of our worst presidents by making him governor) made me just cringe when I heard that Houston's entry into the NFL was to be called the Texans. And not only is the nickname arrogant, it is also lazy and uncreative. At least with nicknames like the 49ers, Packers, and Steelers you learn a little about the local community and history. You learn nothing about the "Texans" other than the people in the state in which the team is located are self-centered. As soon as it was announced, it shot to the top of the list of worst nicknames in the NFL.

I hate the Houston Texans.

AFC SOUTH

Indianapolis Colts

The decade or so from the early '90s to the beginning of the new century was generally a time of relative optimism for Vikings fans, and not without good reason. This stretch of ten or so years, otherwise known as the Denny Green era, certainly produced its share of success. There were a handful of division titles, additional playoff berths, and two appearances in the NFC Championship Game.

While it was generally a time of optimism, the Denny Green era was also a time of tremendous upheaval and change within the Minnesota Vikings organization. There were, of course, the usual types of changes that any franchise experiences during the course of a decade: coaches and players moving on for various reasons, shifts in ownership, and so on. But a much more fundamental change occurred under Green's watch. The Vikings became an offensive-oriented football team.

For the majority of the franchise's history, the Vikings' reputation was built on the defensive side of the football. Minnesota did have its share of stars on offense: Fran Tarkenton, Ahmad Rashad, and Chuck Foreman to name a few. But the Vikings did not come to be known as the Purple People Eaters because of Tarkenton's scrambling, Rashad's soft hands, or Foreman's bruising runs. The Vikings came to be known as the Purple People Eaters because men like Carl Eller and Jim Marshall and (my favorite) Alan Page would routinely schedule conferences at the opposing team's quarterback to be held shortly after the snap. And when the other team's poor schmoe under center would manage to get a pass in the air, Paul Krause and his brethren often knocked it down or picked it off.

The original Purple People Eaters were a bit before my time. Nonetheless, their legacy lived on after they retired. I grew up watching almost equally tremendous defenses lead by men like Chris Doleman, Keith Millard, and Joey Browner. The Vikings of those days did not have much offense of which to speak, but that hardly mattered. They could, and often did, win games on the strength of their ferocious defense.

That all began to change when Denny Green became head coach in 1992. That year's most memorable contest may have been the last hurrah for the Vikings as a defensive-oriented team. The similarly situated (and thus equally offensively challenged) Pittsburgh Steelers were able to fend off the less-than-mighty forays of the Vikings' offensive unit for most of the game. That is until two fourth quarter field goals produced a 6-3 Vikings victory.

From that moment forward, the Vikings slowly became a force on the offensive side of the football. It was a gradual transition at first, but with a little help from Randy Moss the Vikings became an exceptionally gifted offensive team. The apex, of course, was 1998 when the Vikings scored an all-time record of 556 points in a single season. Even after 1998 the Vikings could be counted on to be explosive and score points in bunches.

Unfortunately, the Vikings increasingly could be counted on to give up a ton of points as well. The legacy that was started by Page, Eller, Marshall, and Krause that was handed down to Doleman, Millard, and Browner was foolishly trusted in the not-so-sure hands of the Jeff Bradys, Ramos McDonalds, and Wasswa Serwangas of the world. Vikings' games became increasingly exciting, with both teams scoring tons of points. But they also became doubly frustrating. A team as capable as scoring as many points as the Vikings from 1998 until early into the new century should have won many more games than it ultimately did.

The end result, of course, was no Super Bowl and no Super Bowl appearances. Denny Green was fired late into the 2001 season, having developed a reputation for coaching the brand of football that could be successful in the regular season, but would not succeed in the playoffs. The old adage that "defense wins championships" seemed all the more true in the wake of Green (although, ironically enough, none of those legendary Vikings' defenses were able to win it all either).

About the same time that the Vikings were descending into mediocrity and worse at the end of Green's reign, the Indianapolis Colts were starting to become much more of a force with which to be reckoned in the AFC. Peyton Manning, who was drafted number one overall in the same year the Vikings took Randy Moss with the twenty-first pick, was rounding into his own and starting to stake his claim as the best quarterback in the NFL. With Marvin Harrison and Edgerrin James, the Colts' "triplets" caused fits for the league's defensive coordinators. Eventually the Colts would come to be coached by a former Vikings coordinator, Tony Dungy.

The irony of that situation is, of course, that Tony Dungy had been the Vikings' defensive coordinator and had presided over the last of the decent Vikings' defenses. Yet there he was in Indianapolis, coaching the same brand of football that was to get Denny Green fired.

Tony coached it better, though. This became starkly apparent on a Monday night in 2004 when the Vikings visited Indianapolis to tangle with the Colts. The game was, inevitably, a shoot-out. In the end, however, the only real surprises were that the teams only combined for fifty-nine points and the Vikings had tied the score with about three minutes left in the game. While scoring a late touchdown in front of a hostile crowd on a Monday night certainly seemed like an encouraging sign in the moment, by that time the Vikings' defense had descended into such a large and putrid cesspool of its own lack of talent and heart that any true fan could have predicted the outcome. The Colts drove rather easily for a game-winning field goal and took their rightful mantle as the best offense in the NFL.

The game was not only significant for this symbolic passing of the torch, it was significant for what it told Vikings fans about Red McCombs and Mike Tice. Both of those gentlemen will earn their proper due in this project. Suffice it to say for the time being that the Monday night game in Indianapolis was an eye-opening event for me. That night made it clear that Tice, in his third full year as head coach, was no better at rallying his players or of designing and sticking to an organizational philosophy than he had been on day one. It was also clear that McCombs, whose whining for a new stadium and threats to move the team were both as constant and irritating as mosquito bites in the summer, was not prepared to spend the money to obtain a competitive coach, players, facilities, or amenities necessary to build a winning team. That night the Colts made me realize just how much of the last half of my precious twenties I was wasting with this team.

At the time the one consolation that I could take from the game was that the Colts, although playing it at a higher level than the Vikings, were still playing the Vikings' system. And, as I had thought, Denny Green had proven that a team cannot win with a powerhouse offense alone. I felt a little bad for Tony Dungy, as he seemed like a decent enough fellow and I liked him when he was with the Vikings. But it was just too bad because defense won championships, after all.

Then they proved the old adage wrong. In one sense I was happy that the Colts won Super Bowl XLI, because that meant that the Bears did not win it. As they are in the top three of my least favorite teams, I consider any success that the Bears have as a personal affront to me. For that reason, the Colts victory was better than the alternative. However, it was merely the candy coating on an otherwise bitter pill. The Colts were able to accomplish what Denny Green and the Vikings were not able to do. They won with a stellar offense and, at best, a mediocre defense.

Denny tried that formula for a number of years. He came close a couple of times, but ultimately never got to the Super Bowl, let alone won one. A lot of Vikings fans were convinced that Denny failed because his basic philosophy was flawed. Denny's downfall was that he did not stick to the adage. He tried to outscore everyone all the time and many (myself included) believed it simply could not be done.

Those Vikings fans (myself included) were wrong. The Colts showed that you did not necessarily need a stellar defense to win it all. The Colts defense played well in their championship run, but Peyton Manning and his brethren on the offensive side of the ball still dictated the course of events for the team, as they had for almost a decade. Or, for just about the same amount of time that Denny Green tried to do the exact same thing in Minnesota.

I hate the Indianapolis Colts.

AFC South

Jacksonville Jaguars

These are the things I DO NOT believe about former Minnesota Vikings head coach Mike Tice:

- His birth name was Juanita Oprah McGillicuddy
- He once ate an entire hippopotamus in one sitting
- He enjoys strangling puppies with his bare hands
- He was a competent head football coach

I think that it is relatively uncontroversial to state that we live in a world where privacy is becoming a rarer and rarer commodity. What with the cell phones with pictures and video and the internet becoming increasingly commonplace it seems that people, particularly public figures, are less able to move about the community without having some video of themselves on somebody's website.

I mention this for two reasons. First, I find it a bit lamentable. I am not convinced that the world needs forty million websites showing pictures of the latest young, female celebrity showing off her hoo-ha in public. Second, I think we, as a society, are creating a culture where it has become more and more acceptable to gossip about others and pass along unsubstantiated rumors. This very much includes the world of sports.

While Mike Tice was coach of the Minnesota Vikings, I would hear the occasional rumor about him. As I have absolutely no way of verifying any of these rumors and, because I do not particularly care if they are true or not, I am not going to bother with committing them to paper.

Rather, I am going to go with what I know. Mike Tice seemed like a nice enough fellow when he was with the Vikings as both a player and as a coach. It certainly seemed like he loved his family, as he would often mention them on his weekly radio show. Among the list of things that I do not believe about Mike Tice is that he is an inherently bad or evil person. However, there are some things that I DO believe about Mike Tice:

- He often exercised poor judgment while he was head coach of the Minnesota Vikings
- He was seriously overmatched during his entire tenure on the job
- He had a strong desire to be liked by his players, the fans, and the local media, which occasionally clouded his judgment and caused him to engage in ridiculous behavior
- He spent one awkward Thanksgiving in his mid-teens trying to find a secluded spot in his grandparents' house where he and his cousin could make out

All right, I do not actually believe the last one on that list. I completely made it up and it is not true. Nonetheless, I do firmly believe the first three points on the list. Let us take one stark example to show why I believe all three: the Randy Ratio.

For those who might not remember, the Randy Ratio was supposed to be the solution to one of the Vikings' major problems. Near the end of Denny Green's tenure as coach there was much grumbling about how the Vikings did not get the ball into the hands of Randy Moss, by far their best playmaker, nearly enough. In an effort to rectify the situation Mike Tice declared, in one of his first statements as the newly appointed head coach, he would make sure he got the ball into Randy's hands on at least 40 percent of the Vikings' offensive plays. Thus was born the Randy Ratio.

I will admit right here and right now that I am not a coach. I do not have extensive coaching experience. Nor do I ever plan on being a coach. But I am willing to go out on a limb and declare that telling your future opponents, along with the rest of the world, what your game plan is going to be is not a winning strategy. I will concede that the other teams in the NFL probably knew that Randy Moss was going to be a big part of the Vikings' offense anyway. Yet, knowing what percentage of the plays are going to one player must have made it easier to game plan

The worst part is that Tice actually seemed to take the Randy Ratio seriously. Had the Randy Ratio been a bit of subterfuge intended to distract the rest of the league, it may have been clever. Maybe. However, often that season one was left with the distinct impression that the Vikings were forcing the ball to Randy Moss and that opposing teams knew it was going to happen. Eventually even Tice conceded that the Randy Ratio was a poor idea.

Nonetheless, the Randy Ratio neatly summed up what was to be the entirety of Mike Tice's coaching career and the three things I believe about him. It was an example of poor judgment, it was a reflection of just how much he was overmatched, and the Randy Ratio also seemed as if it was created to garner the support of fans (which was sad and misguided in and of itself because there were many Vikings fans at the time who believed that the team was engaging in an injustice when they were not throwing the bomb to Randy on every play).

Were the Randy Ratio a lone example of Tice's ineptitude as head coach then it could easily be dismissed as a rookie mistake. But it was to be the first in a pattern of stumbles for Tice and the franchise. There were the draft day blunders, the almost criminally inept clock management, the interminable challenge flags, the late season collapses after fast starts, the ticket scalping affair, the lack of discipline for wayward players, the sniping with the media, and so on. It was a comedy of errors that finally just turned into a tragedy. Thankfully, finally, mercifully, after four-plus years Mike Tice was let go by the Vikings.

What, you may ask, does all of this have to do with the Jacksonville Jaguars? How does an extended discussion of Mike Tice reveal this Vikings fan's hate for the Jaguars? After all, the Vikings and the Jaguars have only played each other three times, with the Vikings winning twice. The most memorable matchup of the three was a contest in 1998 when it looked like an injured Randall Cunningham would be unable to take the field against the Jaguars. A clearly happy Jay Fiedler was interviewed by the local media in the middle of the week. It would have been Fiedler's first NFL start had Cunningham not "miraculously" recovered in time to play the game. Cunningham, by that point in life, was a born again Christian and gave all of the credit for his speedy convalescence to the Almighty.

As bad as it looked for the Vikings in the week before the game, things were much, much worse for the Jaguars. Due to various injuries, it would be the Jaguars who would give their young, third-string quarterback his first NFL start that week. Jonathan Quinn started under center for the Jacksonville and was nearly as putrid as the many puns about Eskimos that the local sports media tried to make out of his last name. Although Minnesota started slowly, they finished with a flourish scoring five touchdowns in the second half en route to a 50-10 victory.

Thus the question remains. How could I hate the Jacksonville Jaguars, especially with their limited history against the Vikings? The answer is relatively simple. They hired Mike Tice.

Mike Tice was not just bad at his job, he was almost purposefully terrible. He was a buffoon who roamed the sideline with a pencil behind his ear and a look of weary unease, as if he understood that we could all see that he was not a good head coach. And he did not get any better. The position of head coach in the NFL is assuredly stressful and carries more worries and difficulties than one must realize. As such, one has to accept that a rookie head coach is going to make a few mistakes as he is learning on the job. However, the key to being successful is to learn from those mistakes. Mike Tice seemed wholly incapable of this type of learning. Two and three and even four years into his stint as coach Tice was still putting his foot in his mouth or covering up for some player who was in trouble or scalping tickets or asking Randy Moss to call into his radio show to prove that everything was all right between the player and the coach only to have Moss make it worse with his own ridiculous comments. Eventually it became clear to anyone paying attention that the Vikings were not going to improve under Tice. His reign as head coach would account for nothing more than killing time. Fall Sundays became a parade of lost hours of precious life on this earth.

I decided on the day when Tice was finally let go that I would immediately detest any team that hired a man who had stolen all of that time of my quickly fading youth. Not long thereafter Jack Del Rio, the former Vikings linebacker and current coach of the Jaguars, hired Tice as an assistant head coach in Jacksonville.

I hate the Jacksonville Jaguars.

AFC SOUTH

Tennessee Titans

The Tennessee Titans began their NFL existence as the Houston Oilers. The nickname "Oilers" was a solid choice for the folks of Houston and the baby blue and red color combination were a unique contribution to the league. Then they moved to Tennessee, changed their name to the Titans, and were eventually replaced by the Texans. By virtue of moving from Houston and thus inflicting the dumbest nickname in all of professional sports upon the world, the Tennessee Titans are easily worthy of hate.

But this is only partially the reason why I hate the Tennessee Titans. I also hate them because in the moment of their greatest success, they became a horrible reminder of one of the worst periods of my life.

I am not sure why I got the feeling I did in the early fall of 1999, I just remember that I did. I was watching some highlight show recount all of that Sunday's action. It was only the second week of the season. Nonetheless, after watching the Titans' highlights, I knew that they were Super Bowl bound that year. I told a friend to watch out for them and about my premonition. He scoffed a bit and wondered how I presumed to know such a thing after only two weeks of football.

My premonition would turn out to be correct. The Titans made their lone Super Bowl appearance that season. The road through the playoffs was not without its bumps, however. In fact, it looked like the Titans would not make it out of the wildcard weekend that year. The Buffalo Bills scored with just sixteen seconds left to play to take the lead on the road. It took an amazing kickoff return, including a perfectly executed lateral from Frank Wycheck to Kevin Dyson (yes, it was a lateral, Bills fans) to snatch victory from the jaws of defeat. The play, now known as the "Music City Miracle," is rightfully considered one of the most amazing plays in NFL history.

That year I was back in my hometown of Grand Forks, North Dakota, during the Super Bowl. I was visiting some friends who had recently had their first child. I was fortunate enough to be able to hold the newborn throughout the course of the game, despite the fact that the mother was concerned that I might leap out of my chair during an exciting play and fling her new daughter into the air and toward some untold fate. I knew better, however. I knew I could control my emotions for a game between two relatively uninspiring teams in a year where I was even more bitterly disappointed than usual that the Vikings were not participating (although not as much as '98).

For the vast majority of the evening the baby was perfectly safe in my arms. This included the exciting conclusion when the Rams were able to keep the Titans about a yard short of tying the game in the waning seconds. The only time the baby was in any trouble was when the viewing audience was treated to a shot of Titans' offensive coordinator, Les Steckel.

The thing about head coaches is that (unless you are in Pittsburgh) they come and they go. And while not all have success, it is reasonable to assume that they all tried to have success to the best of their abilities. Spending any unnecessary amount of time or energy hating your team's former coaches is generally a waste. You might rightfully hate a particular decision (why did you take that knee, Denny?) or you might give them a passing harrumph, but unless they were particularly inept or downright disgraceful, they are generally not worth it.

Although none have accomplished the ultimate goal, the Vikings have generally had coaches who, in retrospect, seemed as if they were at least competent. Bud Grant, of course, was a very successful coach. Jerry Burns did the best he could and had some success himself, as did Denny Green.

Some coaches, however, just stick in your craw. Mike Tice was an overmatched lunkhead who routinely embarrassed the organization. While time has healed whatever wounds that were inflicted by Grant, Burns, and Green, I am hard pressed to imagine a future where I will ever feel like the Mike Tice era was anything other than a complete debacle. Yet, despite his seemingly weekly effort to earn the crown, not even the mighty exploits of the Randy Ratio, draft day fumbles, and ticket scalping could earn Tice the distinction of worst coach in Vikings history. That inglorious title has, and forever will, belong to Les Steckel.

Steckel's lone year at the helm for the Vikings in 1984 coincided with one of the most difficult years of my young life. My parents had divorced the year before and my mother moved my sister and myself from our hometown of Grand Forks to Minot, North Dakota. I do not blame my mother for moving us, as she was pursuing an opportunity for herself to better our lives. Nor was moving a particularly rare experience for my family in my eight years on the earth.

Nonetheless, the move to Minot was tough. Not only was I changing schools (again), I was leaving my father, my grandparents, and all of my friends back home. Whereas in Grand Forks I had my own bedroom, in Minot I had to share a room with my sister. There were plenty of other injustices I felt back then, none worthy of recounting in the here and now. Suffice it to say that it was a lonely, unhappy period of time that mercifully ended when we moved back to

Grand Forks about a year later.

That fall I could have really used some success for my favorite football team. They were not obliging. Bud Grant, who by that time had been coaching .500 football for about half a dozen years, retired the previous year. Steckel was something of a surprise hire, and one to which the team would not react positively. The whole thing blew up in Steckel's face and the team woefully limped to its worst record ever at 3-13. Steckel was gone after that and the players could not have seemed happier to see him leave.

It was a horrible year only made worse by a horrible football coach inflicting a horrible record on my favorite team. Since that time I have never been able to find it in my heart to forgive Steckel for what he did to the Vikings that season. He seemed to disappear into the night after that. He, as far as I have ever known, has never come close to a head coaching job since. I thought that he was gone from my life forever.

But I was not rid of Les Steckel. As I sat there watching the Super Bowl, holding a newborn infant in my arms, I was brought back to those painful days in Minot. I was shocked beyond words to see that Steckel was still around, let alone handling a position as important as offensive coordinator for a Super Bowl participant. I might have understood if he was the coach of the waterboys or something of the like, but offensive coordinator? For a team in the Super Bowl? I knew right then and there that the Titans would lose. They not only brought it upon themselves, they brought me back to those terrible days in Minot, North Dakota.

I hate the Tennessee Titans.

AFC EAST

Buffalo Bills

So, what do you think about when you think about the Bills?

I am sure that if you took the time to consider Buffalo's NFL franchise, you would eventually start to think about a young team that is beginning to show some promise, even though they are stuck in one of the tougher divisions in the league. And maybe you might think about some of the greatest players to don the Bills uniform. Men like Jim Kelly and Thurman Thomas and Bruce Smith were among the giants of the game when they played. Or, perhaps if you were of a different generation, you might remember some of Buffalo's earlier all-time greats, like Jack Kemp and O.J. Simpson. As infamous as Simpson is now it is almost possible to forget that he was the first player in NFL history to rush for 2,000 yards in a season. Even more impressive, the league only played fourteen games in the regular season back then. Or perhaps you might ruminate upon the fact that the Bills were originally an AFL team and helped, with their AFL counterparts, to crack the monopoly the NFL held on professional football and opened up the game to a looser brand of play.

Perhaps you might end up thinking about all of those things. But seriously, what is the first thing that comes to mind when you think about the Buffalo Bills? It has to be the four consecutive Super Bowl losses.

I will never forget what happened with the Denver Broncos in the wake of Super Bowl XXIV. The Broncos immediately became the butt of all of the jokes about NFL futility. Their 0-4 Super Bowl record was presumed as the ultimate reflection of a team that could not get it done.

The only problem was that the Vikings were the first team to suffer that ignominy. After the Broncos lost their fourth Super Bowl, people actually forgot that the Vikings had done it first. This was a sore spot for me and for other Vikings fans because going 0-4 in Super Bowl was, in many ways, the only claim to fame or greatness that the Vikings had. Losing four Super Bowls may have been a lousy record to own, but at least it was some sort of record. Many of us felt that, as long as we had those losses, at least we had something. And, after Super Bowl XXIV, the Broncos were taking that away from us. It was quite sad, actually. During that stretch of time I would catch myself reminding people who were making fun of the Broncos that my favorite team was the first to suck that bad.

In the wake of Super Bowl XXIV, I–and many other Vikings fans–found myself having to defend the honor of the Vikings' dishonor. Little did any of us know that it would only get worse. The year after the Broncos lost their fourth Super Bowl, the Buffalo Bills played in their first. It was an especially memorable game that might be rightfully called the greatest Super Bowl ever played. The New York Giants used a bruising running game to keep the especially high-powered Bills offense off of the field. When the Bills did have the ball, the Giants played eight men in the secondary. They were willing to concede, and did concede, huge chunks of yards to Thurman Thomas to keep Jim Kelly and his receivers from making big plays. Despite this strategy, the Bills had a chance to win it in the end. They, of course, did not win. Scott Norwood barely pushed a forty-seven-yard field goal to the right of the goal posts and the Giants escaped with a 20-19 victory.

That bitter defeat was the first of four. Three short years after Norwood's miss the Bills would join the Vikings and the Broncos in the 0-4 club. Four consecutive Super Bowls, four consecutive losses. Each one was worse than the last. The fourth Super Bowl loss was especially terrible to watch for two reasons. First, it was the lone rematch from the previous year's game. In Super Bowl XXVII the Dallas Cowboys would crush the Bills and in Super Bowl XXVIII they would do so again. Everybody who had bothered to pay attention to even a reasonable amount of football during that period of time knew what was going to happen. It was nowhere close to fun to watch.

Second, that fourth Super Bowl loss cheated the football public out of the Super Bowl that it really wanted to see. One of the more intriguing plotlines in the late '80s and early '90s was the quarterback controversy in San Francisco between Joe Montana and Steve Young. The controversy would not end until a seemingly past-his-prime Montana was traded to Kansas City. It would turn out, however, that Montana still had a few good years left in him. The 49ers were not too shabby with Young at the helm either. Both the Chiefs and the 49ers made their respective Conference Championship Games that year. Had both teams won, the sporting public would have been treated to a truly intriguing matchup of the all-time great seeking revenge on the man who replaced him and the team that let him go. Alas, they both lost and the sporting public was left with the previous year's nausea-inducing leftovers.

The end result of it all is that the Bills began replacing the Broncos (and, consequently, the Vikings) as the NFL's symbol of futility even before they lost their fourth Super Bowl. When they did lose that fourth consecutive game, they almost completely replaced the Broncos (and, consequently, the Vikings) as the butt of all of the jokes. Four years after the Bills were beaten by the Cowboys (again), the Broncos completely removed themselves from such conversations by winning it all, and then winning it all the next year as well. When it was all said and done, the Bills, rather unquestionably, earned the title of the biggest losers in the biggest game.

This is personally disheartening for me as a Vikings fan. Those four Super Bowl losses were an unlikely source of pride for us. And when the Broncos lost their fourth we could still make cogent (and, I continue to maintain, accurate) arguments that the Vikings did it with less flair or competency. We were bigger losers.

Not now. The Bills completely outdid the Vikings. Four Super Bowl losses is tough, regardless of the circumstances. But to do it in four consecutive years? That is just brutal. While the second, third, and fourth Super Bowls were uncompetitive, that first loss was the kind of game that rips out your heart and never puts all of it back again.

The Vikings have had some tough, tough losses in the history of the franchise. Some games are impossible to forget ('98 NFC Championship Game, anyone?). But their Super Bowl losses were all uncompetitive. They never had a Norwood-esque moment on the game's biggest stage.

Prior to the Bills, the Vikings could rightfully claim to be the game's biggest loser. Not now. Not anymore. Four years and a forty-seven-yard missed field goal have undercut the validity of that assertion. As sick as it was, it was the Vikings' source of pride. The Bills ended that.

I hate the Buffalo Bills.

AFC EAST

Miami Dolphins

Another AFC traditional powerhouse, another team that shellacked the Vikings in a Super Bowl. This particular whipping was the second of the four losses and was as decidedly uncompetitive as the others. The Vikings never lost a Super Bowl by fewer than ten points. The victory was the second consecutive for the Dolphins and it came a year after their perfect season of 1972. The loss in Super Bowl VIII also made the Vikings the first two-time loser of the big game.

Yet, as with the Raiders (and with the Steelers, for that matter) I do not hate the Dolphins as much as I probably should for that Super Bowl loss. The game was played almost two full years before I was born. I do not mean to imply that I do not hate the Dolphins for vanquishing the Vikings that day in January of 1974. Any self-respecting Vikings fan has to hate them for that. Rather, I am merely stating that my hate for the Dolphins stems from not just that Super Bowl beatdown. It also stems from three other sources: Dan Marino, Cris Carter, and Daunte Culpepper.

Let us start with Marino. In one sense, Marino is a tragic figure, which should, one would believe, make him impervious to hate. When he retired he was numerically the greatest quarterback to ever play the game, holding every meaningful season and career passing statistic. He may not hold many of those records for much longer, what with the increasingly clownish Brett Favre attempting to limp past him and with Peyton Manning showing absolutely no signs of slowing down (Manning has already taken Marino's single season touchdown mark). Regardless, when Marino hung up his cleats his name was at the top of all of the lists for quarterbacks. Yet, Marino was never able to achieve something that Favre and Manning, and several other lesser players at his position (Mark Rypien, Trent Dilfer, and Doug Williams for example), were able to achieve. Marino never won a Super Bowl.

It was an unfortunate example of the best not being quite good enough. In many ways, it is the archetypical tragic sports story: an athlete who rises above the rest to achieve all of the personal accolades possible is cursed with having never won the sport's ultimate prize. It did make Marino a sympathetic figure. However, it also became why the Dolphins are hateable.

As his career continued and the possibility of never winning a Super Bowl became more and more real, the sporting public was forced to endure a constant barrage of stories about Marino's lack of success in the playoffs and his dwindling chances to win the big one. It started off as a yearly question. "Is this the year Marino and the Dolphins [it was never just the Dolphins, it was always Marino and the Dolphins] finally win it all?" Then, as Marino got older, the tone of the questions changed. It became "Will Marino ever win a Super Bowl?" and "Can he ever earn the capstone to his great career?" And as the questions became more desperate and grating, they also became more frequent. The yearly question became a weekly question, even in the offseason as well, it seemed. Enthusiastic announcers never missed an opportunity to mention the hole in Marino's resume at the intro to every Dolphins game and whenever they found themselves needing something to talk about during a lull in the action.

The archetypical story became typical. And then it became a crutch for lazy sports media members who did not want to bother with coming up with a fresh angle. Every story about a backup tight end's injury focused on how it would affect Marino's chances at a Super Bowl. Or how the new food in the concession stand might change Marino's game plan in the playoffs. Or was it possible that the gloves he gave his linemen was what kept him from winning the big one?

Finally it became annoying and unavoidable. For at least the last half dozen or so years of his career everyone who mentioned Dan Marino had to mention the asterisk on his list of accomplishments. Everyone had to point out that he was a tragic hero. Ultimately Dan Marino cannot be blamed for how the sporting media unceasingly described his career and accomplishments, and lack thereof. Undoubtedly he was sick of it as well. But that does not change the fact that it happened. It made Dolphins games unwatchable and worthy of hate.

The trouble with the Dolphins did not quell when Marino retired. Those lazy sports journalists simply shifted their focus from Marino's Super Bowl chances to who would replace Marino. This unfortunate trend was still in effect (as it seems to be to this day) when Cris Carter joined the Dolphins three years after Marino's retirement.

Carter, of course, spent the bulk of his career in Minnesota amassing hall of fame–worthy statistics. He had been cut from the Philadelphia Eagles three years into his career by Buddy Ryan, who famously and stupidly stated that the rationale for his decision was because Carter "only catches touchdowns." There was, however, some method to Ryan's madness (in this one, very limited instance). Carter had admitted to traveling a dark path with illegal substances during his Philly days. Perhaps Ryan wanted to rid himself of his self-destructive player before something terrible happened; Carter himself has often stated that getting cut was what turned his life around. Not long thereafter Carter found the Lord and turned himself into one of the greats in the game and the best player on either side of the ball for the Vikings for a good, long time.

Carter was generally a hero in the community during his time in Minnesota. But he also had a penchant for pouting and for being preachy. These faults were overlooked by Vikings fans when he was putting up Pro Bowl numbers on a yearly basis. Yet, when the production dropped and he was a clear second option to Randy Moss, those same characteristics quickly became unbearable. When Carter was let go by the team in 2001, the general mood of Vikings fans was to thank Cris for his many years of tremendous service to the team, but to also remind him to make sure the door did not hit him on his backside on the way out.

Carter did not stay on the sidelines, however. Like a good number of athletes, Cris decided that leaving the game with a modicum of grace and dignity was no way to end a career. He found a desperate taker in the Dolphins around midseason and was injured early into his time with the team. He came back from injury, but ultimately Carter's eight catches for sixty-six yards that season did little to alleviate the worry about who would replace Dan Marino.

Seeing Cris Carter in a Dolphins uniform was relatively sickening. He should have just left Minnesota with a smile and a wave and rode off into the sunset. Instead, he decided to give his legacy one good, hard, swift kick while it was briefly down. Despite this, Cris Carter is not the most infuriating former Viking to don a Dolphins uniform after his Minnesota playing days. That distinction belongs to Daunte Culpepper.

Not everyone remembers that when it became clear that the Dolphins were no longer going to employ the services of Dan Marino, the Vikings made a hard push to get him to sign with the team. The thinking was that Marino would provide a year or two of competent quarterback play and tutelage to his young understudy. In the end, Marino decided to forgo the chance to spit on his reputation in the same way that Cris Carter would readily accept three years later. Without a suitable veteran option, the Vikings went with their second-year quarterback: Daunte Culpepper.

Daunte preformed admirably that first year. The team, as a whole, was somewhat up and down. Yet they battled all the way to the NFC Championship game, where they were then thoroughly trounced 41-0 by the Giants. Nonetheless, the future looked very bright. The Vikings were blessed with an unstoppable tank at quarterback in Daunte and the most dangerous offensive weapon in the game in Randy Moss. If two players with so much talent could not lead the Vikings to the Super Bowl, then no one could.

Maybe no one can. Randy had his well-chronicled problems. Daunte, for his part, was a model of inconsistency. Pro Bowl years would be followed by indescribably hideous years. Sometimes Daunte would pinpoint passes as if he were using a laser and sometimes he would fling the ball in the air as if he were playing a game of 500. Daunte did not attract as much negative attention as did Randy for his attitude and behavior, but perhaps he should have. There was one incident where Daunte's vehicle was shot at and involved in a chase after he and some other folks had been at a club that was also open to eighteen- to twenty-year-olds. He also had a one-day holdout from training camp (that no one was willing to admit was a holdout) to protest his contract.

The last straw for Daunte and the Vikings came when Daunte, after suffering a serious knee injury against Carolina during one of his down years, fired his agent, decided that he was going to be his own agent, and demanded a ridiculous new contract. He began sending emails directly to the local media. He then asked for a trade, which, of course, only harmed his trade value and the ability of the team to move him. Nonetheless, the Vikings were able to oblige him and shipped him to Miami for a second round pick.

The entire incident reflected a lack of maturity on Daunte's part. In retrospect, much of Daunte's career revealed a high level of immaturity. The inconsistency and the pouting and the ridiculous orchestration of his eventual trade were not the actions of a man who had fully grown up. And, any man who could not properly handle the relatively minor adversity (for an NFL quarterback) that Daunte faced in Minnesota is certainly not the kind of man who could quarterback a team to a Super Bowl championship.

Randy left the Vikings before Daunte. And he took his half of the promise that the two of them held for Vikings fans. With Daunte still on the team many Vikings fans (myself included) believed that there continued to be enough talent to have success on the offensive side of the football. But it turns out that Daunte was not up to the task. Miami's orange and blue number eight is a symbol of the dead hope that stemmed from two of the most talented and immature players to ever wear the purple and gold.

I hate the Miami Dolphins.

AFC EAST

New England Patriots

Here is the deal with sports talk radio. It is a proven scientific fact that prolonged exposure to sports talk radio will eventually make you stupider.

Sports talk radio in relatively low doses, scientists have determined, generally does not lead to permanent damage, particularly when there is actual sports news worthy of discussion. The problem, medical science generally agrees, occurs when there is little to no news to discuss. In these not-so-rare instances of twenty-four-hour, seven-days-a-week, 365-days-a-year sports talk radio, time must necessarily be filled in some manner. The solution to the time-killing dilemma is usually to manufacture some sort of debate or make some relatively trivial point a product of intense discussion.

Debates in sports are not rare. In fact, they can be quite fun and, for decades, have produced lively discussions at the corner bar, around the water cooler, and whenever a group of folks want to talk about something just for the heck of it. Who was a better centerfielder, DiMaggio or Mays? If you had the choice for your NBA franchise, would you prefer Russell's defense and knack for winning or Wilt's sheer dominance? Who would win the dream Super Bowl, the Steelers of the '70s or the 49ers of the '80s?

These types of discussions can be good for you and rarely ever end in decreased intelligence, particularly when the debating parties do not take themselves too seriously. The problem, the scientists tell us, is when the participants become sanctimonious and treat these essentially meaningless discussions as if they were life and death.

Therein lies the danger of sports talk radio. Because sports news ebbs and flows with a fair amount of unpredictability, sports talk radio hosts oftentimes have to create conversation. While this process in and of itself does not have to be dangerous, it becomes so when that conversation carries a level of importance far greater than that of which it is capable of carrying. It is not enough for these talk show "personalities" to defend their choices of DiMaggio, Russell, and the '70s Steelers, they must do so as if they were defending the pearly gates from the hordes of the underworld. And, precisely because these folks are "personalities," they refuse to waiver from their stated position, lest they deviate from their "image."

It is listening to those sorts of things that makes a person stupider. Some people are so affected by sports talk radio that they are willing to believe that they can accomplish something by calling in to a show. For as much sports talk radio I have listened to and for as much as it has chipped away at my intellect, I have still never been able to convince myself that calling in was a good idea. Nor do I understand why anyone else would think it is a good idea. Most callers to sports talk radio have clearly flown off the handle about something that was said and are usually too worked up to express a coherent thought. And those rare callers who do have a salient point are generally cut off by the "personality" who does not want to deal with reasoned logic and does not have to do so because she or he controls the access to the airwaves. It is a losing proposition.

So, the bottom line is that sports talk radio makes you

stupider. And sports talk radio thrives on manufactured debates. One such debate of relatively recent vintage has been whether Bill Belichick and Tom Brady's Patriots are a dynasty. Some say that, particularly in the salary cap era of the NFL, the success that the Patriots have had qualifies them for dynasty status. Others state that New England needs to stretch their period of success over a greater period of time to truly earn the dynasty tag. Usually these folks also want to claim that the Patriots of today would not hold up against the juggernauts of the past.

It is these others who are wrong. Three Super Bowls in four years is a remarkable, almost unparalleled accomplishment. Their continued success after those Super Bowls, even though it has not resulted in additional rings, is one of the hallmarks of a dynasty. And they still yet may win more. Besides, if the coked-up jailbirds who played for Dallas in the early '90s can be a dynasty, then the Patriots have to qualify as well.

So, is this why I hate the New England Patriots? Is it because they have produced an inordinate number of mindless debates on sports talk radio in recent years? Well, sort of. But the more real reason why I hate the Patriots is because before they began having all of this success in Super Bowls, they had a tremendous amount of failure.

Bill Belichick, Tom Brady, and the rest of the crew in New England with the three Super Bowl trophies have made a lot of people forget that the Patriots have actually played in five different Super Bowls. Before all their glorious success, the Patriots were two-time Super Bowl losers.

And who did the Patriots lose to before beginning their victorious rampage through the game's biggest stage? First it was the Chicago Bears in Super Bowl XX and then the Green Bay Packers in Super Bowl XXXI. Chicago and Green Bay are permanent residents in my top three hated football teams of all time.

Neither Super Bowl loss was particularly pleasant. In fact, Super Bowl XX was foregone conclusion before the opening kickoff.

It only became a bigger and bigger joke from that point forward. The Bears were nearly unstoppable that year, losing only once in the regular season. That loss, to the Dolphins in Miami, remains the highest-rated *Monday Night Football* game of all time (as one is reminded every time the Bears or the Dolphins have appeared on *Monday Night* since). The playoffs would prove to be no different. The ten points that the Bears gave up to the Patriots were the only points they would give up in the postseason. The forty-six points they scored in opposition to New England's ten quickly turned the game into a route. Even worse, those Bears created an unholy, Frankensteinish mixture of music and sports known as the "Super Bowl Shuffle." It is, quite possibly, the worst collection of sounds and noises to ever earn the label of "music." And it paved the way for other unfortunate productions by athletes who wanted to test their mettle in the recording studio. The whole collection of goofballs that Bears team sported, from head coach Mike Ditka to the allegedly "punky QB" Jim McMahon on down to William "The Refrigerator" Perry, were a despicable lot who made a young Vikings fan's life miserable in some of his earliest years.

Super Bowl XXXI was no picnic either. While the game managed to remain relatively close very briefly into the third quarter, Desmond Howard's ninety-nine-yard kickoff return after a New England touchdown killed any New England momentum or hope for the rest of the game. Green Bay would cruise to a two-touchdown victory and a whole new generation of Packers fans became exponentially more annoying. The most played highlight of that particular game was an exuberant Brett Favre running about the field holding his helmet aloft. Assuredly it was a crowing moment for him not just because the Packers would win the Super Bowl, but because an overanxious collection of folks in the sports media (and more than a few Green Bay fans, I might remind you) were already questioning whether Favre had what it took to quarterback a championship team.

The game was even more excruciating for me because that was the first year I was living in the twin cities and attending the

University of Minnesota. The twin cities and the U attracted a rather sizable share of Wisconsin citizens who, all of the sudden, bought a bunch of Packer paraphernalia and claimed their die-hard allegiance. Where all those hats and jackets and jerseys were when Forrest Gregg was coaching and Randy Wright was quarterbacking the team I will never know. In any event, the seemingly new crop of Packers fans wearing packers garb became a constant reminder of the hated rival's success and the Vikings lack thereof.

The Patriots deserve their due as the NFL's most recent dynasty. They are a good team lead by an excellent coach and quarterback. But before they found championship glory, two mediocre Patriots teams weaseled their way into the Super Bowl and dropped lopsided contests to the two biggest rivals of the Vikings.

I hate the New England Patriots.

AFC East

New York Jets

For the vast majority of their existence, the New York Jets have been generally terrible. The franchise has been around for over forty-five years and only has four division championships and eight playoff wins (compared to eleven losses) to show for it. The '70s were a barren wasteland for the team. While they fielded some decent teams in the '80s, those teams never amounted to much in the playoffs. Since about the mid-1980s it was another long stretch of nothing for the Jets. Then they kind of turned it around. Sort of. In the last ten years or so there has been another small, and relatively unimportant, collection of successes. A Super Bowl appearance has been, more or less, out of the question for nearly forty years.

This less-than-glorious history should, one might assume, make the Jets unhateable. Particularly for a Vikings fan. And yet, I do hate them. I hate them for two reasons.

The first reason that I hate the New York Jets is that they have something that no other franchise in the history of professional football will ever have. The Jets have Super Bowl III.

By now, anybody who has cared about the NFL at any point in time in the last forty years knows what happened in Super Bowl III. The Jets, then of the AFL, were huge underdogs to the veteran, seemingly invincible Baltimore Colts of the NFL. Two AFL-NFL World Championships (Super Bowl III was actually the first time the two leagues called the game the "Super Bowl") had been previously played, with the Green Bay Packers emerging victorious in both contests. Many folks were still convinced at the time that the AFL was the NFL's junior varsity and stood no chance of ever winning a game against the big boys.

But this was the '60s. And, as the baby boomers like to try to convince us every single chance they get, everything changed in the '60s. Of the many tales told about Super Bowl III (and tales aplenty have been told), most like to contextualize the game as not just a contest between two rival leagues, but as also a generational war that reflected that turbulent time in American history. It was the upstart, free-wheeling, hairy Jets versus the staid, disciplined, crew cut Colts. It was young versus old, change versus consistency, hippies versus squares.

The face of those hairy Jets was, of course, Joe Namath. Broadway Joe was no shrinking violet in the spotlight, and he would add plenty of fuel to this supposed generational fire. Namath, above all of his other accomplishments, is most famous for guaranteeing that his underdog Jets would be victorious. Of course, Namath would not be nearly as famous if he and the Jets had not delivered on his guarantee.

The lore that has been built around Super Bowl III has obscured the fact that it was not a particularly good game. The Jets were able to build a 16-0 lead into the fourth quarter on the strength of a second quarter touchdown and three subsequent field goals. The Colts tallied the final score of the game, but their lone fourth quarter touchdown would not be nearly enough to emerge victorious. The footage of Namath wagging his index finger in a "number one" salute as he is running off the field is one of the most famous Super

Bowl shots of all time and propelled Namath into the level of athlete superstardom.

The Jets won the game, the hippies won this battle in the generational war, and the AFL would win the respect of the sporting public. It was, in many ways, a watershed moment for all of football and some have argued that it was the most important football game ever played. Perhaps it was the most important football game ever played and perhaps it was not. But it is most certainly the reason why the Jets are worthy of hate.

Has one franchise ever coasted on one championship for as long and as strong as the Jets have coasted on their victory in Super Bowl III? Seriously, this has generally been a terribly run franchise with a gaggle of mediocre to bad players. And yet, whenever anyone thinks about the Jets they immediately think about Super Bowl III. It was the one shining moment in an otherwise craptastic team history. When one looks at the big picture, one is forced to recognize the Jets as a stumbling collection of generally useless, club-footed imbeciles. And, upon closer inspection, even Joe Namath does not seem so great. The man threw forty-seven more career interceptions than touchdown passes after all.

The part that is even worse for a Vikings fan is the fact that the next year's upset of an NFL team by an AFL team was no big deal. The Vikings entered Super Bowl IV as thirteen-point favorites over the Kansas City Chiefs. Despite those cheery prognostications, the Vikings would fall to Kansas City by sixteen points. It was the first of the four Super Bowl losses and, because of the Jets and their upset, perhaps the most forgotten. If it were not for the NFL Films program of the game, featuring Kansas City coach Hank Stram jumping around and making funny noises like a child's toy, maybe nobody outside of Kansas City and Minnesota would remember the game.

After Super Bowl IV the NFL and AFL completely merged into one league. Thus, in many ways, the Vikings losing Super Bowl IV was the last official act of the NFL as its own league. This fact is not given nearly enough due. And it is all because of the New York Jets' one shining year amongst around forty-five or so bad to marginally passable ones as a professional football franchise.

So, the Jets are hateable for that reason. But they are hateable for one more reason as well. They are kryptonite to the Vikings. The Vikings have a winning record over seventeen of the NFL's franchises. And for thirteen of the fourteen other NFL franchises the Vikings either have an even record against them or have at least something close to an even record. This is not so with the Jets. The Jets have emerged victorious in seven of their eight contests with the Vikings. How and why the Vikings so consistently crumble like a house of cards when facing the Jets I will never know. All I know is that the traditionally putrid Jets own the purple and gold. The Vikings' 1-7 record against New York is by far their worst against any team.

I hate the New York Jets.

AFC North

Baltimore Ravens

I suppose I would be remiss if I failed to mention somewhere in this project that I do hate it when a team decides to move. The brain wizards who are paid to make such activities more palatable to the public often call this process "relocation." I call it a loathsome act by which a greedy owner rips the heart out of a fan base in order to turn her or his multi-millions into more multi-millions. I also hate the brain wizards. Without getting into a lengthy screed about euphemisms and/or political correctness, I do think it is worth pointing out that one of the most effective uses of language is as a tool of manipulation. The same folks who call moving a team "relocation" are the same folks who changed what happened before the start of the regular season from "exhibition games" to "pre-season football" in order to sell more tickets. Be wary of the language you use and the language you hear.

Having made that point and having climbed down off the soapbox, I now want to make a confession. I do not hate it when a team moves as much as I probably should. I suppose it is because over time things seemed to have, more or less, worked out. During the course of my life there have been six NFL franchises who have packed up and moved from one city to another. Yet, five of the six cities to have lost a team, Baltimore, Cleveland, Houston, St. Louis, and Oakland, have eventually regained an NFL franchise. One of the group, Oakland, got the same franchise back and another, Cleveland, managed to keep a hold of the ugliest uniforms in the league, so it is kind of like they got the franchise back. And the only team to still be missing out on the NFL, Los Angeles, does not seem to care at all.

I suppose I mention all of this because there is a part of me that wishes I hated the Baltimore Ravens more for participating in the various team swapping of the last twenty-five years or so. The franchise was born as the original Cleveland Browns before moving to Baltimore, changing their team name, uniforms, and color scheme, and replacing the Colts, who had moved out of town about a decade earlier. By all accounts, the original Browns fans and Baltimore Colts fans were loyal, passionate, and devastated when their teams left town. Thus, it almost seems like the Ravens should be doubly hateable for their involvement with two NFL-spurned cities. But they are not. At least not from my vantage point.

Rather, my hate for the Baltimore Ravens is much less selfless and much more superficial. I hate the Baltimore Ravens for their coach and their uniforms.

As you may have deduced by this point (assuming that you have been reading cover to cover), 1998 was, for me, both the best and (by far) the worst year to be a Vikings fan. Perhaps the man most responsible for this, even more so than head coach Denny Green, was offensive coordinator Brian Billick. The 1998 season has been and will continue to be given its due over the course of this project. Suffice it to say that the 556 points the Vikings scored that season made the vast majority of the year extremely fun to watch.

The season did not end well, however. Again, that story will be given its due at the proper time. What is important for the time being is that Billick left after that season to become the head coach of the Ravens. The Vikings offense continued to be good after Billick's departure. But they were never again great. Randall Cunningham, whose '98 season might best be characterized as supremely efficient, reverted back to his typically erratic self in '99 without Billick and he was eventually replaced by Jeff George.

Two years later the sports world was almost treated to one of those classic (or perhaps clichéd, depending on your disposition) matchups in the Super Bowl between mentor and student. The Vikings had fought their way through an up-and-down season in which they won their first seven contests but also lost their last three regular season games to cough up the number one seed in the playoffs. This meant that the Vikings had to go on the road to face the number one seeded New York Giants in the NFC Championship Game. It was nothing close to a contest. The Giants cruised to the Super Bowl by demolishing the Vikings 41-0. The biggest fight the Vikings put up all day was when Randy Moss yelled at a security guard who refused to allow some of Randy's friends on the field before the game.

Had the Vikings not laid that huge goose egg in the middle of the New Jersey swamp where Giants Stadium is located, they would have faced Billick and the Ravens in the Super Bowl. However, there was no guarantee that it would have been anything closer to a decent game than the NFC Championship Game had been. The Ravens won that season, ironically enough considering Billick's background, on the strength of an all-time great defense. The Vikings, by that time, were living off of the fumes of the offense Billick had helped put together.

Billick and the Ravens won it all that year, dominating the Giants in a rather uninspiring game. It would be a harbinger of things to come for Denny Green's main assistants. Tony Dungy's Super Bowl victory would come after the 2006 season. Dungy was actually the first to leave, in 1996. His recent success has made a lot of folks forget that he was the man behind Tampa Bay's brief surge into the NFL's elite. While Jon Gruden was the coach to win the Super Bowl, that squad was still very much Dungy's team.

Vikings fans were leery when Dungy left. A few years later many were downright despondent after Billick left. In both cases several fans believed that the team had erred by letting the assistant go and keeping the head coach. It turns out that those fans may have been right in both cases. The 2000 season became a clear example of just how valuable assistant coaches can be.

However, missed opportunities with assistant coaches is not the only reason I hate the Baltimore Ravens. I also hate them because they have removed some of the distinctiveness of the Vikings.

The brain wizards who alter our language in an effort to manipulate us do not stop with the words we speak. They also have changed the things that we look at. This includes team uniforms. Nowadays uniforms are created by corporate mandates with the intention of pushing as many jerseys and caps as possible. That is why almost every team that has switched uniforms or added an alternate uniform in the last twenty years has made black a dominant color.

It used to be, however, that uniforms were a unique expression of a franchise and the city in which it was located. Teams were not only not afraid to be different, they actively sought out a way to be distinct. The Tampa Bay Buccaneers are the perfect example of this trend and how it completely went by the wayside when the brain wizards gained a tighter hold over the sporting world. The Bucs began their life with two different shades of orange as their dominant colors. Whatever one might have thought about those uniforms, there was no mistaking when you were watching a Tampa Bay game. Yet, the Bucs would eventually give up their unique contribution to sports fashion for (in my opinion) even uglier uniforms that follow the well-trod path of corporate blandness.

The Vikings, for all of their many faults, have more or less stayed true to their distinctive style. The purple jerseys and helmets have always been an immediate and sure sign that the Vikings were playing. Yet, through no fault of their own, the Vikings lost a little of that distinctiveness when the Ravens decided to make purple one of their dominant colors. Whereas once the Vikings could claim this obscure (for the sports world at least) color for their own, now they have been forced to share. This is not right. Purple should belong to the Vikings. If you follow one of the loser teams that claims red or blue or black as one of its dominant colors then you should be prepared to share with the rest of the uncreative simpletons. But if you proudly claim a color as off-beat as purple for your team, then you should get it for team and your team alone.

I hate the Baltimore Ravens.

AFC NORTH

Cincinnati Bengals

Failure is bad. Failure hurts. Perhaps the greatest fear in all of humankind, the one fear that has been the cause of more suffering, angst, and hand wringing than any other, is the fear of failure.

And yet, it is inevitable. Much like death, one day we must all face failure. It is part of the human condition. It is such a part of our lives and our experiences that we build great stories about moments of failure. Sometimes we tell stories of failure as a precursor to stories of success. And sometimes we tell them to remind ourselves of the devastating effects of bad habits such as ill-preparedness or hubris. And sometimes we tell stories of failure for our own amusement, whether it be a simple attempt to gently tease ourselves or our loved ones or a more sinister attempt to revel in the misery of others.

Quite often that moment of failure can be very revealing. Sometimes it is a turning point in which one decides to take charge and change her or his life for the better. Sometimes it can be the proverbial straw that beaks the camel's back and sends a person tumbling toward an unfortunate end. Moments of failure can also be quite unifying. Who among us has not wanted to console a child who struck out in the last inning of his little league game or did poorly on an important test in school? And who among us would not be willing to throw an arm around a buddy and buy that person a beverage at the local watering hole on the day that person found out that she or he did not get the valuable promotion at work? And who among us has not needed that consolation from others at some point?

Unfortunately, moments of failure can also be a mirror. And sometimes those mirrors can show you something worse than failure.

The Cincinnati Bengals, by the mid-1990s were a team exceptionally familiar with failure. Their somewhat hasty decline from Super Bowl participant after the 1988 season into the cesspool of NFL bottom feeders had already cost Sam Wyche his job as head coach and was about to cost Mike Shula the very same position. Things had gotten so bad in Cincinnati that 1995's record of 7-9 was a vast improvement for the team. Regardless, this minor improvement did not last long and the Bengals, who had been out of the playoffs for five years by that point, would not find much more success until three head coaches and about a decade later.

As the Bengals were right in the middle of their horrible, fifteen-or-so-year slump, it seemed that they were the perfect opponent for the Minnesota Vikings in the last week of that 1995 season. The Bengals, by that point, had nothing to play for. The Vikings, on the other hand, desperately needed the victory.

The 1995 season, like many before and since, was an up-and-down affair for the Minnesota Vikings. The entire year followed a nausea-inducing, roller-coaster-esque path of wins and losses. The first four games of the season were loss-win-loss-win. In the middle of the season the Vikings followed up three consecutive losses with three consecutive wins. It was dizzying trying to figure out where the team stood in the standings, let alone whether they had any shot of making the playoffs.

As it turned out, as the last week of the season approached, the Vikings did have a chance to make the playoffs. However, they were in the unenviable position of needing help to get there. The Vikings needed both the Atlanta Falcons to lose to the San Francisco 49ers and the Chicago Bears to lose to the Philadelphia Eagles. Most importantly, however, the Vikings needed to take care of their own business and win their game against the downtrodden Bengals.

The Vikings may have been a bit jittery to start the game. By the end of the first quarter, the game was tied with each team only managing a field goal. However, the second quarter was a different story. The Vikings began a three-touchdown scoring stretch in about the middle of the second quarter to take a twenty-one-point lead into halftime. All was well, it seemed. The Vikings, who needed a victory to maintain any playoff hopes, were comfortably ahead of a team that seemed more than willing to roll over and die. San Francisco was also winning at halftime of its game. The only problem was that Philly was down by ten to the Bears at the half of their game. Nevertheless, there was still hope. In fact, there was even more hope when the Eagles recovered a Bears fumble in the end zone for a touchdown at the beginning of the fourth quarter of that game.

Unfortunately, that was also about the time that the Vikings were beginning to unravel against the Bengals. The team that had stormed Cincinnati in the second quarter was apparently still sitting in the locker room when the second half started. The Vikings were unable to maintain the offensive production from the first half and the defense, inexplicably, had been replaced by a collection of statues and pylons. Cincinnati scored two touchdowns in the third quarter to pull the game within seven points. They managed the tying score about midway through the fourth quarter and eventually won the game on a last-second field goal.

The Vikings needed three things to all happen on that Sunday to make the playoffs. As fate would have it, none of them occurred. Not making the playoffs was cause enough for sorrow. However, the spectacular way in which the Vikings threw away a very winnable game was downright disgusting. They did not even bother to give themselves a chance to lament their luck with the other two games. They decided that they would make sure to focus all of the disappointment squarely upon themselves. And what better way to generate disappointment and contempt than by blowing a twenty-one-point lead to a bad team?

Believe it or not, the Vikings found a way to make that loss even worse. On that December Sunday in 1995 the Cincinnati Bengals, generally failures themselves at the time, held a mirror to the Vikings so that the team could get a good look at itself after that loss. The reflection from that day was something that should have made the team ashamed and certainly made many fans cringe upon seeing it.

As bad as the loss itself was, the real ugliness came from the behavior of the team's best player, Cris Carter. The previous year, Carter set the record for receptions in a season with 122. It was during a small stretch in time when the single season mark seemed to be broken every year. And it would be no different with Carter's record. The previous day, Herman Moore of the Detroit Lions had reestablished the record with 123 receptions. Carter, knowing full well that he needed eight catches to tie and nine to regain the top spot was petulant and whiny all day. His body language expressed deep disappointment whenever the team had the temerity to look to any other player but him. Carter would tie his personal best, but his seven receptions that day would not prove to be enough to regain the record. Carter then proceeded to whine about it in the locker room after the game.

That loss to the Bengals reflected who the Vikings were that year. What Vikings fans and the rest of the NFL saw was the best player and team leader much more concerned with his personal accomplishments than with the fate of the team. With that level of selfishness as a guide, the team proved to have no real heart or ability to triumph over adversity. It was an ugly moment of self-realization that made losing a football game to a bad team pale in comparison.

The Bengals showed Vikings fans and the rest of the world just exactly who and what the Vikings were on that December day.

I hate the Cincinnati Bengals.

AFC North

Cleveland Browns

I do not begrudge a man who attempts to help his child to achieve a better place in life. In fact, one might argue that helping your child to succeed is the sole and defining purpose of being a parent. And while I do not currently have any children of my own, I can still empathize with the impulse to encourage and inspire a younger generation to greater heights.

Nonetheless, there is a limit. Sometimes, the "help" that a parent gives to a child ends up being more harmful to the child and to the relationship than if the parent had left well enough alone. We have all seen or heard about (or perhaps even been) that guy who is always pushing his kid to practice and play a sport well past the point of enjoyment. This is the same guy who will complain to a volunteer coach that his eight-year-old is not getting enough playing time. Or maybe it is the exceptionally strict parents who, in an effort to shield their child from the evils of the world, inadvertently push that child to seek out the vices and temptations in life.

At some point, a parent has to make the difficult decision

to let go and to trust the child to make her or his own decisions. Undoubtedly, this is one of the many painful moments that comes along with the duties of raising and nurturing and caring for another human being. But it has to happen. Preferably, the process of letting go and allowing a child to grow into her or his own happens before the child either completely rebels or becomes incapable of handling her or his own affairs. And it certainly needs to happen before the parent and the child are so connected to one another that they almost cripple two different NFL franchises.

This is a lesson that was apparently not learned by Denny Green. Before the 2001 season, which was to be his last as head coach of the Minnesota Vikings, Green orchestrated a series of small trades with the Cleveland Browns. In each instance, the Vikings gave up some low-level draft picks to acquire players from the Browns who were probably lucky to still have any trade value whatsoever. All told, the Cleveland Browns shipped four players to the Vikings. Two of the players, Everett Lindsay and Stalin Colinet, had been with the Vikings before. Colinet, in fact, was well acquainted with the journey from Ohio to the twin cities. He started his career with the Vikings, went to Cleveland, came back to Minnesota, and went to Cleveland for another year before making his third tour of duty with the Vikings. The one player to seemingly hold the most promise for the Vikings was Travis Prentice. While Prentice's 512 rushing yards for the second year, reborn Browns were hardly spectacular, they did lead the team. Nonetheless, Prentice hardly made any impact for the Vikings, amassing a mere thirteen yards on fourteen attempts in 2001.

The final player the Vikings acquired from the Browns in the early fall of 2001 was a quarterback who would make an impact that season. We shall turn our attention to that quarterback in just a moment. Yet, a question lingers: why would the Minnesota Vikings and the Cleveland Browns make a series of trades with one another in the early fall of 2001? After all, by the beginning of the new century trades were a rare event in the NFL. When trades did happen, they were generally concentrated around the time of the draft. Any such activity outside of the draft had become exceedingly rare in the salary cap era.

Yet, the Vikings and the Browns were tossing players and draft picks back and forth like they were jugglers in the circus. How could this be? The answer may have something to do with the lesson that Denny did not learn about letting go.

It turns out that the director of pro personnel for the Cleveland Browns at the time was Jeremy Green, Denny's son. The two must have shared a close relationship as they were on the phone constantly with each other in the early fall of 2001. And, apparently, orchestrating NFL trades was the Green family's version of spending quality time together.

In one sense, the trades, as disturbingly frequent as they were, were relatively harmless. Mediocre players were swapped for players that were to become, at best, mediocre. Were it not for the fact that actual human beings (who had to pick up and move to a new city and everything that comes with that) were involved, it would have been as irrelevant as swapping trading cards. The trades were also some of the last transactions that Denny Green would complete as a member of the Vikings organization.

But, in another sense, they inflicted a terrible injustice on the team. The fourth player to be traded from the Browns to the Vikings was Spergon Wynn. Although Denny had been relatively successful during his tenure, many Vikings fans by that time were anxious to see him go. Poetic justice would have a bit to say in Denny's eventual departure that year. The final quarterback to take a snap for the team under Denny's watch was the second-year quarterback Denny got from his son.

Spergon Wynn was the worst player to ever start a game at quarterback for the Minnesota Vikings. Thanks to injuries to Daunte Culpepper and Todd Bouman, Wynn manned the helm for the final two games of the 2001 season. Ironically enough, Denny was fired with a game to go and Mike Tice would start his coaching reign with Wynn under center. The results were not good. Wynn could not even manage to find a receiver for half of his passes in his three games for the Vikings, finishing with a completion percentage of 49 percent (which, by the way, was a vast improvement over the 40.7 percent of the passes he had completed for the Browns in seven games the previous year). He also threw six interceptions in those three games, as opposed to one touchdown pass. And even those statistics do not tell the full story. The scoring throw itself, which went into the record books as a forty-seven-yard strike to tight end Byron Chamberlain, actually only traveled about seven yards up the field. Chamberlain rumbled the remaining forty yards to the end zone to gift wrap Wynn's only career NFL touchdown pass.

The Vikings would finish 5-11 that year. Those who wanted to see Denny go got their wish. And Spergon Wynn was the final piece of the puzzle. Little did fans realize that Wynn would become a precursor of things to come. By 2001 Red McCombs had gone from the owner/savior who presided over the glorious '98 season to a crazy, cheapskate, dingbat who cared more about a new stadium than producing a quality environment and winning football games. His commitment to pinching every penny lead him to keep the overmatched Mike Tice on as head coach. Spergon Wynn was, in many ways, the perfect quarterback to usher in that era.

Wynn has not taken an NFL snap since that season. The Vikings have become almost as irrelevant since Spergon lead the charge in the final two games of the 2001 season. The worst part is that he should not have even been on the roster. Were it not for the fact that Denny (who was accused more than once during his tenure in Minnesota of being overly loyal to certain coaches and players) was keeping a watchful eye on his son, then Spergon would not have been on the roster.

The Cleveland Browns have been a putridly run organization ever since they rejoined the NFL. And yet, in the fall of 2001, the Minnesota Vikings were more than willing to scoop up as many of their castoffs as they could get their hands on. Denny and Jeremy Green saw to that.

I hate the Cleveland Browns.

AFC North

Pittsburgh Steelers

I suppose that it is fitting that the section on the AFC in this project both (kind of) begins and ends with a discussion of a team that throttled the Vikings in a Super Bowl. Whereas the Kansas City Chiefs had their way with the purple and gold in Super Bowl IV, five years later it would be Pittsburgh's turn in Super Bowl IX. The Vikings would be within a field goal after scoring on a blocked punt in the fourth quarter. However, the Steelers defense held the Vikings to a total of 119 yards for the whole game and a late fourth quarter touchdown sealed the 16-6 defeat.

That championship was the beginning of an amazing run for the Steelers, as they would win a total of four Super Bowls in the span of six years. The Steelers were, unquestionably, the team of the 1970s and some believe that those Pittsburgh teams were the greatest ever assembled.

The loss was the third for the Vikings. The fourth would come two years later to the Oakland Raiders. Three years after that, the Steelers would go 4-0 in Super Bowls, besting the then–Los

Angeles Rams.

Alas, I must again confess to not hating the Steelers as much as I should for the smothering they put upon the Vikings on that January day in 1975. Rather, in the early part of my life I had a much different understanding of the Steelers. The Super Bowl against the Rams occurred shortly after my fourth birthday. During that time the Steelers seemed to be on television almost as much as the Vikings. Being too young to know much of the history of my favorite team, I developed a bit of affection for Chuck Noll's crew. In fact, the first jersey I ever owned was a Mean Joe Greene jersey. My family was able to get it for me by collecting the plastic inserts in the top of soda bottles. Each plastic insert had the face of an all-pro player and if one collected all of the players, one could get a jersey. I seem to recall, even though it has been over twenty-five years now, that we were short a player or two. Nonetheless, I do remember that my dad walked into the place where you redeemed the plastic inserts and walked out with the Mean Joe Greene #75. I was very sad when I eventually outgrew that jersey.

Ultimately, the Steelers were probably my first ever "second team." But then I grew up. And, as happens to us all at some point, I began to lose my childhood innocence and see what the Steelers truly represented to a Minnesota Vikings fan. The Steelers were, in many ways, everything that the Vikings were not.

Of course, the Steelers are different from a lot of teams. They have been owned by the same family since the inception of the franchise. In the summer of 2007 they hired just their third head coach in nearly forty years. Chuck Noll was hired in 1969 and held the post for twenty-three years. Such a gaudy number manages to dwarf even Bill Cowher's remarkable fifteen years at the helm. In that stretch of time when the Steelers have had two head coaches, the Vikings have had six. And six is an extremely mild number by comparison. Excluding a few interim folks, the Cardinals have had eleven coaches in that time, as has Detroit and New England. The record, excluding the interim coaches, appears to lie with the Jets, who have had twelve head coaches in the time that the Steelers have had two.

Another difference emerges when one considers the image the Steelers have around football. Whenever some team wants to claim some sort of identity, it will often state that it is playing its own particular brand of that sport. And when a team is playing poorly it will often claim that it is not performing its brand of the game. Coaches at all levels do this. For example, if your local high school uses the nickname "Spiders" and if you pay attention to the local high school teams you will inevitably hear, at some point in time, a coach say, "We just want to go out there and make sure we play 'Spiders' tennis this weekend" or "we got out of our game plan and we didn't run 'Spiders' cross country at the meet."

In most cases such a claim is just plain foolish. The vast majority of the teams on the sports landscape do not have an identifiable set of characteristics upon which to stake some sort of identity. The local high school cannot participate or deviate from "Spiders" volleyball because there is no substance or meaning behind the term "Spiders volleyball."

This is decidedly not the case with the Pittsburgh Steelers. When one talks about Steelers football some clearly understood images jump to mind. Steelers football involves a downright nasty defense, a punishing running game, a distinct home field advantage, and the ability to play efficiently in any kind of weather.

"Steelers football" also means consistency. The characteristics of Steelers football have not changed for forty years. The entire franchise has maintained a discernable philosophy for at least four decades. This is true not just for the product on the field but also for the way the front office is run. The Steelers have had plenty of good players during their history. But they have always seemed to lack the type of players who thought of themselves as superstars and somehow more important than the rest of the team. Whenever the Pittsburgh franchise did run into one of those characters, he was let go fairly quickly. They have never let one player eat too much of the team's salary cap or the team's glory.

To hold and maintain such a philosophy is very much unlike the Vikings. The Vikings are a team that has held many philosophies during its run as an NFL franchise, had several different owners, and employed all kinds of goofballs who cared more about their paychecks than the good of the team, and have mostly lacked any prolonged institutional consistency.

In fact, for much of my youth the Vikings and the Steelers were parallel opposites. Whereas the Vikings were 0-4 in Super Bowls, the Steelers were 4-0. Whereas the Vikings rather quickly became a soft, dome team, the Steelers greeted the elements as a gift from the football gods. Whereas the Vikings changed coaches, visions, game plans, and personnel, the Steelers seemed to move with an unparalleled unity. The direct comparisons between the two franchises waned a bit when the 49ers won their fourth Super Bowl. Yet, with a Steelers-like consistency, those comparisons had lingered for nearly twenty years.

Through both the good times and the bad, the Pittsburgh Steelers have always been the Pittsburgh Steelers. Through it all they have managed to win five total Super Bowls and, now that they have stolen the Vikings' defensive coordinator Mike Tomlin, they look to remain as Steeler-like and as un-Viking-like as ever.

I hate the Pittsburgh Steelers.

PART II – THE NFC

When I began this project I knew full well that I hated every single NFC team for some reason or another. After all, this is the conference in which the Vikings play and these are the teams with whom the Vikings routinely do battle.

So, I knew it was going to be easy to write a section for every one of the NFC teams. And it was easy. In fact, it was so easy it was hard.

In many cases, there are multiple reasons to hate this or that particular NFC team. My mind began getting soupy trying to sort out all of those reasons. Thus, in an effort to both keep this project at a reasonable length and to keep my sanity, I have, more or less, picked one definitive reason why I hate each NFC team. It is not the only reason why I hate that squad, but it is the reason that best exemplifies why that team is worthy of contempt.

If you are a Vikings fan you will, undoubtedly, be able to think of several reasons to hate, say, the Chicago Bears. And, undoubtedly, those reasons are valid. Please understand that I recognize that there are countless reasons to hate the Bears. I just happened to focus, more or less, on one of them.

Here is why I hate the teams of the NFC

NFC WEST

Arizona Cardinals

Nathan Poole.

The landscape of Minnesota Vikings history is absolutely littered with missed opportunities, blown chances, and squandered possibilities. Should a person ever decide to take a stroll though that treacherous terrain, then that person will inevitably come across the mountainous pile of what-could-have-beens sitting right smack in the middle of the landscape, ruining everybody's view. The bottom line for this franchise is that when they have needed to come up with a clutch performance they have generally found themselves with their hands around their own throats, choking away yet another victory, playoff berth, season, or all three.

Perhaps the greatest reason why the land of Vikings lore is so terribly gloomy is because one of the team's dominant characteristics over the years has been an almost ceaseless ability to play to the level of their competition. This has come in handy at times, when a seemingly overmatched Vikings squad would, at the very least, keep the game close against a superior opponent. They would even come up with an unexpected victory every now and then. However, this has been a terribly annoying characteristic whenever they have played a clearly inferior opponent. Many times the Vikings have let a truly bad football team hold on to hope deep into the fourth quarter. And much too often the Vikings have let that truly bad football team steal a victory.

Before this discussion moves any further, it should be noted that this annoying Vikings characteristic does not apply to Super Bowls.

In any event, this all gets us back to Nathan Poole and the 2003 season. I suppose that any player who has the heart, ability, and wherewithal to make it to the NFL deserves some credit. And Poole did play in the best league on the planet. However, his career is not particularly notable. He has played in thirty-six games over the course of five seasons. His most productive season was in 2003 when he played in fifteen games and made thirteen catches for 177 yards. Poole also scored one of his two career touchdowns that season–a very notable touchdown.

The 2003 season started out brilliantly for the Minnesota Vikings. They won their first six games and seemed destined for a playoff berth, if not more. Mike Tice was in his second full year as head coach and it honestly seemed like he had weathered his stormy first year and was prepared to take a huge step forward. The Randy Ratio was behind him and the future looked bright.

Unfortunately, that bright future turned out to be the light on the front of the train that would smack right into the 2003 season. A loss at home in week eight to the New York Giants was the first of four straight defeats. The rest of the season would teeter back and forth as the Vikings fought to secure the playoff berth that once seemed assured.

It would eventually all come down to the final week of the season. The Vikings and the Green Bay Packers went into that last week with identical 9-6 records. As it stood, only one of the two teams would be able to make the playoffs. The Vikings held the tiebreaker with the Packers so they controlled their own destiny. A victory and the Vikings would have the playoff berth they seemingly could have banked on when they were 6-0.

Even if the Vikings lost, they still would have been able to make the playoffs with a Green Bay loss. But that seemed unlikely as the Packers were hosting the Denver Broncos. Heading into the game the Broncos already knew they were in the playoffs and they knew that their seed in the playoffs could not change. Their biggest goal that Sunday was to make it out of Wisconsin without getting anyone injured.

Thus, everybody knew that the Vikings really needed to win that last week of the regular season. Luckily, the opponent was the Arizona Cardinals who were mired in yet another terrible season. Throughout the entire history of the NFL, the Cardinals can, rather rightly, be understood as the worst team the league has ever produced. The Cardinals do hold the distinction of being the oldest continuing professional football franchise, beginning in 1898. Yet, this long history has only made the team exceptionally acquainted with losing. Their one hundred plus years of existence has lead to over two hundred more franchise losses than victories.

The Vikings would have to play the game in Arizona, but that would be just about the only disadvantage the team would have heading into the contest. The 2003 season was just another redundant chapter in the big book of the Cardinals' losing history. They headed into the game with a 3-12 record and their coach, Dave McGinnis, would be leading the team for the last time that day. A loss and a shot at the number one overall draft pick clearly would have helped the Cardinals more than a victory on that Sunday. The Vikings could not have written a better script for a victory.

Alas, the Cardinals either did not get their copy of the script or they decided to improvise. Either way, a disturbingly flat Vikings squad found themselves trailing by two field goals at the half without having scored any points themselves. Things began turning around at about the middle of the third quarter when the Vikings scored a touchdown to take the lead. Things looked even better when the Vikings scored another touchdown and field goal in the fourth quarter to take an eleven-point lead. The chase had been difficult and victory had been elusive, but it now appeared that the hunt was over.

It was not over just yet, however. The Cardinals scored with about two minutes left and tried a two-point conversion to bring the game within a field goal. When they did not convert, the game really seemed to be in hand for the Vikings. Down by five and with no time to waste the Cardinals did the obvious: they tried the onside kick. The relatively poor success rate of the play belies its desperate origins, but the Cardinals were somehow able to convert. A pass interference penalty, a hallmark of that year's Vikings defense, brought the Cardinals to within striking distance of the end zone, and catch number twelve of Poole's thirteen that year brought his team to the Vikings' thirteen-yard line. Showing a rare bit of heart and success, the Vikings defense sacked Arizona quarterback Josh McCown on the next two plays. It all set up the final play of the game.

The game was played three days after Christmas. As had become tradition for me, I spent the majority of the holiday season in my car, traveling to visit various family members throughout the upper Midwest. On that particular day I was at my father's place, watching the game with my father and some of my siblings. I recall it being a particularly nice holiday season because a young cousin of mine had given me a Vikings hat as a present. My sister and I were her godparents and our cousin always showed an extra level of affection for the both of us ever since she was old enough to realize that we took on that responsibility on her behalf.

So, that year my favorite present was my Vikings hat. I tried to talk her out of buying it for me because it was far too selfless of an act for someone at her tender age and I thought that she should have spent her little bit of money on herself. But she insisted and I was proud to wear it and I will never forget that act of tenderness.

I decided to wear the hat as a good luck charm that Sunday. I figured any gift given with that much kindness had to bring fortune.

As I sat on my father's couch I nervously fidgeted with the hat. The game in Green Bay had finished fairly quickly and as anticipated. In those last few minutes of the Vikings game, the broadcast would cut to a shot of Lambeau Field where the Packers players and the fans watched the end of the Vikings-Cardinals contest on the stadium scoreboard. The Vikings, by that time, had long known that they needed the victory to get into the playoffs. And then it all came down to that one last play.

The ball was on the Vikings' twenty-eight-yard line. There were four seconds left. This one play would determine the playoff fate for two different teams. McCown rolled to his right and fired a desperate shot into the right side of the end zone.

And then it happened. Nathan Poole happened.

Poole caught the ball for the game-winning touchdown. Just like that the season was over. The Minnesota Vikings became only the second team in NFL history to start a season with six consecutive wins and miss the playoffs. The Arizona Cardinals celebrated wildly. The players and fans in Lambeau Field celebrated wildly. The few Vikings fans that the camera could find were standing in disbelief and horror. Nathan Poole ended the season.

The class acts in Green Bay would give Nathan Poole a key to the city the next week. It was the last bullet to the head to the corpse of the Vikings' season. But truthfully, the Vikings should have never found themselves in the position of needing to win that game. Arizona finished the season at 4-12, tied with the New York Giants, Oakland Raiders, and San Diego Chargers for the league's worst record. Minnesota lost to all four of those teams in 2003. Had they beaten just one of the worst teams in the NFL that year they would have gone to the playoffs. Had they beaten all four they would have finished with a 13-3 record and would have had the number-one seed in the playoffs.

But they did not win any of those four games. They managed to maintain their ability to play to the level of their competition and they paid for it. 2003 was, quite possibly, the most Viking of Vikings seasons.

As for me, I jumped up from my seat as soon as Poole caught the ball. I kept perfectly still as there was a brief glimmer of hope while the play was being reviewed. That slim hope died when the referee ruled that Poole had been pushed out of bounds and the touchdown stood. I took the hat off of my head, mumbled a few good byes to my family, and jumped in my car to make the three hour drive back to my apartment in the twin cities.

I have not worn the hat since.

I hate the Arizona Cardinals.

NFC WEST

San Francisco 49ers

Have you ever had a rival who was, plain and simple, better than you? Maybe it was that little redhead back in the third grade. Sure, she was cute (not that you would have admitted it at the time), but she always managed doing better than you on the spelling tests. Or maybe you played for a team in high school that, despite its best possible efforts, was never able to beat the cross-town rival. Or maybe there is some guy at work who manages to get every bonus and promotion that you have ever worked toward.

Jerry Burns took over the reins as Vikings head coach from Bud Grant in 1986. Although Grant was, unquestionably, the best coach in the history of the franchise, by the late '70s and into the '80s he was only able to keep the team hovering around an even record. The first time Grant retired, after the 1983 season, he was replaced by the comically inept Les Steckel. The 3-13 record fashioned by Steckel was the worst in team history and Bud was summoned back for another season to clean up the mess. Grant retired permanently after the 1985 season.

The Les Steckel–lead 1984 Vikings was not only the worst season in terms of the team's record, it was probably also the worst season in terms of the team's attitude. The players did not like or respect Steckel. And Burns, who had been a long time assistant coach under Grant almost left the team when he was passed over for the head job the first time Bud retired. But Burns got his chance after Grant's second retirement.

Burns turned out to be a relatively successful coach. He just missed the payoffs in his first year in the top spot and would make the playoffs in his next three years. The Vikings, who had become used to mediocrity and worse, were finally winning and playing meaningful football games again. Burns was the coach of some of the more successful Vikings teams in their post–Super Bowl era.

And yet Jerry Burns was not able to lead any of his teams to a Super Bowl. He made it to one NFC Championship Game (which will be given its full due in a later section), but that was as good as it got for Jerry's boys. The Vikings, who had once again become meaningful in the mid- to late '80s and early '90s, were unable to make it to the final hurdle, let alone get over it.

The reason why Jerry Burns was unable to take that final step and bring his team to the big game is because he was constantly running into that dreaded third grade girl who is a better speller. The NFC was absolutely loaded with championship-caliber teams in those years, thus making almost all of them like that hated cross-town rival. There were Mike Ditka's Bears and Joe Gibbs's Redskins and Bill Parcells's Giants, to name some of the major villains. During Jerry Burns's tenure as head coach of the Minnesota Vikings, the NFC was right in the middle of a stretch whereby the conference would win fifteen of sixteen Super Bowls, including thirteen in a row.

The biggest winners during that era were the San Francisco 49ers. Their first Super Bowl victory began the NFC's sixteen-year stretch of dominance and the Niners would win a total of five championships within a fourteen-year span. The 49ers were the team of the '80s and the team that was, in many ways, the most vexing during the Jerry Burns era.

By my unofficial count, the Vikings and the 49ers played each other approximately 485 times in the regular season and playoffs during the mid- to late '80s through the early '90s, with the Niners winning 484 of those contests. The Vikings did score one memorable playoff victory against San Francisco (which will be given its full due in a later section), but that was about it. Most of the time, the Niners treated the Vikings like a minor speed bump on the road to more important games and more important opponents.

The entire relationship between the two teams is probably best encapsulated in one play. The game was played on October 30, 1988. The Vikings, who had produced their one victory in 485 tries in the previous year's playoffs during that stretch of time, returned to the Bay Area for yet another contest against the 49ers. The Vikings entered the game at 5-3 and really could have used the victory at the time.

Things looked good for the Purple for the most part. Minnesota still had a stout defense at the time and went into the half with a 7-3 lead. From that point forward the game bounced back and forth. The Vikings' third quarter touchdown was sandwiched by two San Francisco touchdowns. The end result was that the Niners had a 17-14 lead heading into the fourth.

The Vikings, who still had their share of heart and guts during the Jerry Burns era, took the lead once again on a characteristically bruising Rick Fenney twelve-yard touchdown run. I remember being tremendously excited at the time. The Vikings had taken a four-point lead and put themselves on the verge of slaying Goliath for the second consecutive game. Having made it to the NFC Championship Game the previous year, another victory would not only have helped a somewhat shaky record, it would have also given the Vikings the psychological advantage that the Bears and the Redskins and the Giants and especially the 49ers had held over them for a number of seasons. They looked like they were ready to kick a huge hole though the glass ceiling that separated them from the NFL's elite teams.

Alas, the glass ceiling was to remain intact. Steve Young made sure of that. As the game was drawing ever near the final gun, Young took the snap, looked around for a while, and then made one of the greatest runs, if not the greatest, by a quarterback of all time. It went down in the scorebook, coincidentally enough, as a forty-nine-yard touchdown scramble. But anyone who watched the game remembers that between both running over and eluding would-be tacklers and zig-zaging from sideline to sideline, Young probably ran closer to 400 yards. Various estimates on how many Vikings had a chance to tackle the San Fran quarterback ranged between and unconscionably low four to a probably-a-little-too-high nine. At the very least, six or seven (and maybe more) of the Vikings players on the field for that play had a shot at Young. An exhausted Young stumbled around the two yard line but still got in to the end zone. There were still nearly two full minutes to play when Young scored, but the game was effectively over. A very good Vikings squad suffered yet another loss to a great team.

The Vikings did rally somewhat after the game. They strung together enough victories to finish 11-5 and make the playoffs as a wild card. Unfortunately, they would run into the 49ers yet again. This time, the game was nowhere near as close as the Niners romped their way to a 34-9 victory. San Francisco went on to capture the third of their five Super Bowls that year.

Jerry Burns coached a handful of really good Vikings teams. Unfortunately, his teams played in a conference with a handful of great teams. The Vikings really did give it their all in those years. And they came close. But they never could take that next step into the NFL's upper class. There was always a rival to stand in their way. During the Jerry Burns era the biggest bully was the team from the bay area.

I hate the San Francisco 49ers.

NFC WEST

Seattle Seahawks

There was a time, when I first started watching football, when the Minnesota Vikings were known for their defense. Although they were a bit before my time, the original Purple People Eaters were able to put the fear of the Almighty into opposing offenses. That reputation carried beyond the Super Bowl years. Even though I never got to see guys like Page and Eller and Krause, I did grow up with the Dolemans and Millards and Browners of the world.

Denny Green slowly but surely changed all of that, although not necessarily for the worse. While the dominant defenses of my youth were no more, the Vikings became a phenomenal offensive team. Led by Randy Moss, and eventually Daunte Culpepper, thirty or more points each and every week seemed like more than a possibility; it seemed like an inevitability.

Of course, the tradeoff was that the defense slipped. For one glorious season in 1998 it seemed like the Vikings had it all. The offense, lead by a rookie Moss, a still valuable Cris Carter, a resurgent Randall Cunningham, and Robert Smith at his peak, scored a record 556 points for the season. The defense, lead mainly by the frenetic John Randle, was opportunistic and was able to capitalize on the mistakes of the opponents' offenses because those offenses often found themselves down two or three touchdowns before they blinked.

It was not meant to be in 1998. Nonetheless, that year was notable for many reasons, including the fact that it marked the real turning point for the Vikings and their identity as a franchise. Whereas once the Purple could smother another team into submission, they now were attempting to outrun, outpace, and outscore the opposition. In the wake of 1998 they continued to be reasonably successful at lighting up the scoreboard. But they were never able to achieve the same level of success as they had managed in '98. And the defense kept slipping. Eventually, trying to outscore the opponents was not just a game plan, it was a method of survival. Too often, the team needed every one of the several points it scored. By the end of Green's run in Minnesota, the formula was no longer viable. The Vikings did not succeed at scoring enough and the defense could not stop anybody.

Thus entered Mike Tice, who promised to bring a blue-collar mentality to the team (all the while also stating that he was going to make sure that Randy Moss touched the ball on 40 percent of the offensive plays). The defense, we were told, was going to improve and become a marker of pride once again. Tice assured an anxious fan base (many of whom were still uncomfortable with the switch from a defensive-oriented philosophy to an offensive-oriented philosophy) that he had a vision and a direction for the team.

Tice was given the difficult job of cleaning up the mess when Green had been fired with one game left in the 2001 season. Understandably, that game resulted in a loss. Nonetheless, the change at the top produced a certain level of excitement among Vikings fans, many of whom believed that Denny was the source of all of the team's ills. Lots of folks were genuinely excited about Tice and the upcoming 2002 season.

That excitement was fairly quickly tempered when the team began the season with three straight losses. Many of the folks who had been happy to see Green get fired were willing to give Tice the benefit of the doubt, but people were beginning to itch for a victory.

It was under these circumstances in which the Vikings made their way to Seattle for a Sunday night game against the Seahawks. For whatever reason, a group of people I knew were excited enough about the contest to make their way to a local bar to watch the game. The establishment was one of those smoky dives that are populated by the working class and the bohemians who love to watch the working class.

So I went along. And, for whatever reason, I got excited about the game. I was not one of the folks who seemed to believe that by virtue of having a new coach the Vikings' fortunes were destined to improve. In fact, I thought that Denny had been treated a little unfairly during his time in Minnesota, especially toward the end (although he did bring much of it on himself). But maybe I got caught up in the undercurrent of that feeling and I went to the smoky dive bar having talked myself into believing that the Purple had a shot. A long shot (I was not delusional, after all), but a shot nonetheless.

Sitting together around a couple of tables, my group of folks and I were very psyched up for the game. The excitement died a swift and painful death. The Seahawks waltzed the ball up the field as if they were practicing drills in training camp. The Vikings displayed a remarkable inability to force the Seattle offense into any sort of difficult position. By the time the first quarter was halfway over, Shaun Alexander had two touchdowns and the Vikings were already in a multiple-score hole. It only got worse. Minnesota was able to put ten points on the board before the half, but it was no match for the four additional touchdowns the Seahawks would score in the second quarter. Alexander himself accounted for five of those first half touchdowns and the sixth came by way of an interception that was returned all of the way. Whatever hope or anticipation that bar held at the start of the night, it was long gone after that first half.

Although I did not pay that much attention from that point on, I seem to remember that, in an effort to remain injury-free, the Seahawks only played seven men on each side of the ball in the second half. And most of those players were people from the stands who had worn jerseys to the game. Even if my memory on that situation is not completely accurate, it did not matter. The Vikings were unable to amount much of anything in the second half either, despite the fact that the Seahawks became completely uninterested in scoring any more points.

The loss dropped Mike Tice's career record up to that point to 0-5. After the game the especially twitchy and reactionary fans were getting riled up at the new coach. In retrospect, they were right. While I only had a vague understanding of what was happening at the time I was watching the Vikings getting pummeled by the Seahawks, I have since come to understand that it was another watershed moment for the franchise. The Vikings had become nothing.

For the first twenty-five or so years of the team's history, they were defined by their defensive prowess. During the Denny Green era they were an offensive juggernaut. Each philosophy had its pros and its cons and each was successful in its own right (even if neither led to a Super Bowl victory). But in either case, at least they were something. The team the Seahawks played that night, and consequently the teams that Mike Tice would coach from thereon in, were nothing. They had no philosophy. They had no identity or defining characteristic other than dysfunction.

This became more and more clear as time went by. Seemingly every couple of weeks Tice would announce a new vision for the squad. Sometimes they were going to grind it out. Sometimes they were going to air it out. Sometimes they were going to attack on both sides of the ball. Sometimes they were going to take what the other team gave them. It was always something new. And each time it was going to answer the critics and be the new identity of the team.

It never worked. Coordinators would come and coordinators would go. Sometimes the Vikings would try new plays to attempt to shake things up. And sometimes they would simplify the playbook to make sure everybody was on the same page. It was one miserable, uninspired adjustment after another.

All the while the Vikings lost whatever identity they had. A lot of people were able to convince themselves for a long time that the Vikings were still a force to be reckoned with on the offensive side of the football in the post-Denny years. But the results do not really bear that out. The Vikings did push the ball up and down the field with a fair amount of frequency, but they had more and more trouble punching the ball into the end zone. Field goals became a staple, and even they got more and more rare until finally the Vikings were just bad on both sides of the ball.

A once proud defense had long been a thing of the past. Now the offense was gone as well. The Vikings were nothing during the Mike Tice era, unless confused and aimless can be considered proper philosophical guides for an NFL franchise. The Sunday night game in Seattle was the first real glimpse of that loss of team identity that would plague the Mike Tice years. The Seahawks showed us what was to come.

I hate the Seattle Seahawks.

NFC West

St. Louis Rams

I am going to come right out and make a statement that will assuredly be controversial amongst many Minnesota Vikings fans. Denny Green was a good football coach.

The general consensus among Vikings fans still seems to be that Denny Green was anywhere from a lackluster to a terrible coach. This is simply not true. I am perfectly willing to concede that Denny did have his faults. He was not necessarily the best game day coach out there. Clock management probably was not a strength. Nor did he get the team to the Super Bowl.

But he was a good coach. Not a great or superior coach, but a good one. His teams did have their share of success. He guided his squads to two NFC Championship Games, four division titles, and eight playoff appearances in his ten years as the leader of the team. A lot of other less capable and less successful people were given the reins to an NFL franchise while Denny was going 97-62 in Minnesota. The Cincinnati Bengals, in Dave Shula, Bruce Coslet, and Dick LeBeau, employed three of them. Green got a lot more criticism from the fans and local media than he deserved while he was the head coach of the Minnesota Vikings. Any lingering Denny haters out there need to find some perspective and recognize that he was not nearly as bad as you seem to want to remember.

Having made that statement, it is also important to note that Denny had a knack for making it very difficult to feel any sense of empathy for him.

All coaches engage in some version of coach-speak. Fans and media members routinely hear the same sorts of meaningless and inane things from coaches. Whenever the team is playing poorly a coach will spew a collection of empty clichés such as "we need to take better care of the ball" or "we just have to take it one game at a time." When things are going well it is along the lines of "We have to keep doing what we do best" or "we just have to take it one game at a time." When a coach wants to deflect attention away from his own ineptness or lack of ability it is something like "We didn't execute like we wanted" or "we just have to take it one game at a time."

Most coaches are fluent in coach-speak. Some are only able to communicate in that language (which has to make you wonder how their home life operates: Wife – "What do you want for dinner, dear?" Coach – "I think we need to get back to doing what we do best. We've been trying to get a little too fancy with the duck l'orange and the tofu stir-fry. We're going to trim down the cookbook and get back to the basics. We have to take this one serving at a time."). Occasionally you will get a bit of genuine information, wisdom, or humor, but those instances are few and far between. Even the most colorful coaches use coach-speak a majority of the time.

This was the source of Denny's biggest problem as coach of the Minnesota Vikings. He was exceptionally poor at coach-speak. This is not to suggest that he was more honest and more forthright with the fans and the media than his contemporaries. He was not, and he attempted to be as guarded and controlling as the rest of the coaches in the league. Instead, he was like a tourist in a foreign land who knew the proper language of the country but was unfamiliar with the vernacular, colloquialisms, and slang of the local community. Thus, like the tourist who inadvertently insults her or his hosts, Denny would often say things that translated poorly to the people and press of the twin cities.

One coach who may have been a bit underrated for his ability to speak both within and without the boundaries of coach-speak was Dick Vermeil. It was this skill that made him a very good football announcer. His success in the television ranks was the primary reason why so many people were stunned when he decided to return to the sidelines with the St. Louis Rams in 1997. After two seasons it looked like Vermeil had made a poor choice. His 9-23 record in those two seasons had many suggesting that the game had passed him by. To make matters worse, Vermeil's starting quarterback for the 1999 season going into training camp, Trent Green (who they acquired from Washington after the Redskins traded for Minnesota's former starter, Brad Johnson), got hurt in the preseason and would be out for the year. I remember distinctly thinking, as I watched a snippet of Vermeil's press conference announcing that Trent Green would be out for the season, that he was as good as gone after that year. I also thought that Vermeil's claim that the team would be all right without Trent Green was nothing but the emptiest form of coach-speak.

Vermeil, it turns out, did leave at the end of that year, but not without collecting a Super Bowl ring first. The completely unknown Kurt Warner was given the starting job and would explode onto the scene with such ferocity that he would be named both MVP for the season and in the Super Bowl. It was the berth of what was nicknamed "the Greatest Show on Turf." Warner, with his amazing wide receiver corps and the newly acquired Marshall Faulk, were next to unstoppable.

The Vikings, on the other hand, were coming off of the disappointment of the 1998 season. Although still a good offensive team, they were not what they had been the previous year. Without offensive coordinator Brian Billick, who left to become the head coach in Baltimore, Randall Cunningham struggled and was replaced by Jeff

George. Although supremely talented, and with an absolute cannon for an arm, George never stayed with any franchise for more than four years and actively sought his way out of a few situations. Despite the fact that he put up very good numbers, the Vikings seemingly did little to secure his services at the end of the season.

The end to the Vikings' 1999 season would come, coincidentally enough, against the St. Louis Rams. While the Vikings did go 10-6 that year, they would lose the division to the Tampa Bay Buccaneers and had to play in the wild card weekend before heading to St. Louis to match up with the 13-3 Rams.

The game was reasonably close for a while. Minnesota drew first blood with a field goal in the first quarter, but St. Louis responded with two touchdowns. Despite the deficit, the Vikings were able to score two touchdowns of their own in the second quarter to take a lead into halftime.

Then it all blew up. The Rams scored on the opening kickoff of the second half, took the lead for good, and never looked back. The Rams scored five straight touchdowns from that opening kickoff of the second half into the fourth quarter to take a thirty-two-point lead. The Vikings managed to score three touchdowns in the final five minutes of the game, but it was far too little, far too late. The final score of 49-37 only served to mask the vicious throttling St. Louis gave the Vikings. The Rams had the both the better offense and the better team that year.

It was another painful loss, particularly in the wake of 1998. While the '98 season undoubtedly spoiled fans, that does not change the fact that the entire '99 season felt off-kilter and destined for failure. And then came the Rams, who were not only playing the same brand of football as the Vikings, but they were doing it better and they would come to have more success.

The final insult in that let-down of a year was when Denny once again flubbed his way through some coach-speak. Denny claimed that the Vikings had not so much been beaten by the Rams, as they had run out of time to catch up to them. This is patently untrue.

The Rams were simply better that year. Whatever his motivation, whether it was to attempt to console his team and the fans, or to deflect attention away from a squad with some growing holes on defense, or to try to light a fire under his boys for next year, the words that came out of Denny's mouth were just plain dumb. Monumentally dumb.

Denny Green was a good coach, but he often said things to make you forget that fact. The Rams, who ended up playing a better brand of Vikings football that season than any of the Vikings teams of that era, provided him with that golden opportunity to stick his foot in his mouth. Denny, as he did too often, obliged.

I hate the St. Louis Rams.

NFC SOUTH

Atlanta Falcons

1998.

A large part of me would like to leave this section as it stood before this paragraph as I am fully aware of the fact that, if you are a Vikings fan, I do not need to do anything more than commit "1998" to paper to explain to you why I hate the Atlanta Falcons. You know what that season meant. You know what happened. You know the heartache that can be caused by the right feet of two foreign-born men. You know. You just know.

But there is the possibility that you are not a Vikings fan. And while you may be cognizant of the fact that the Atlanta Falcons defeated the Minnesota Vikings in overtime in the NFC Championship Game on January 17, 1999, you do not know. I really do not want to do this. I wish I could erase it from my memory. But I will share it with you anyway because you do not know.

With all due respect to the teams that made it to the Super Bowl, this was the best Minnesota Vikings team to ever take the field. The '98 team would only lose twice in the eighteen games that the squad played. No other Vikings team can make such a claim. And they were loaded with players who either had career years or were so good that each season was like a career year.

They had a rookie Randy Moss, who had not yet decided that he was only going to play when he wanted to play. Cris Carter was still an exceptionally productive receiver. Robert Smith was not only healthy, he had the most carries he ever would in a season and had his second of four consecutive 1,000-yard campaigns. Randall Cunningham played at an MVP level. The team scored a record 556 points for the season (which, coincidentally enough, seems like the 556th time I have mentioned that fact in this project).

On the defensive side of the ball, John Randle, who would make the Pro Bowl for the sixth consecutive time after the '98 season, led a stout group, including Ed McDaniel, Robert Griffith, and other solid performers. They were opportunistic, they provided additional opportunities for the offense by creating turnovers, and they also managed scoring their fair share of those 556 points.

The season started with five consecutive wins before the bye week. There were a couple of close shaves in those first five weeks, including a three-point victory over Chicago. After the bye the team was nothing short of superior. The Vikings did lose their lone regular season game to the Tampa Bay Buccaneers in week nine. Yet, that was the only blemish in those final eleven weeks. They absolutely obliterated their opponents. Only one other foe after the bye, New Orleans in week ten, kept the game within double digits.

The team was unstoppable, as was the buzz in the twin cities. Everybody was excited about the Vikings. People who never cared for the sport in previous seasons were curious to know what the score of the latest game was. Complete strangers would strike up conversations about the team. No interaction in the twin cities, whether it be the most mundane or the most deeply serious, was complete without some mention of the Vikings. Everybody was nicer and friendlier and more willing to be considerate and helpful. It truly affected the entire mood of the community and it affected it completely for the better.

I have never been happier as a fan. Each Sunday provided a joyous occasion for three hours in the afternoon in the form of a football game. The rest of the week was merely an excuse to review what had happened. Although the Vikings had made the playoffs in the 1997 season (and in five out of the six seasons before '98), there was little indication that the magic of '98 was about to occur. There was a decent amount of buzz when Randy Moss slipped to the twenty-first pick in the draft and the Vikings were able to snatch him up, but no one knew the effect he would have on the team. Nor was anyone able to predict Randall Cunningham's stunning emergence into the quarterback that Philadelphia had desperately wanted him to be for so many years, despite the bit of success he had for the Vikings in '97.

A friend and I had decided to buy a partial season ticket package for Vikings games that year. We got the "cat" package, which got us tickets to games against the Lions, Bengals, and Jaguars. The Vikings won all three of those games by a combined score of 103-16. We could not have been more ecstatic when the order form for playoff tickets arrived in the mail. Despite the fact that money was tight (and we both were kind of cheap), we filled it out and sent the checks immediately.

The first playoff game was over before it started. The Arizona Cardinals were making an extremely rare appearance in the postseason. They had beaten the Dallas Cowboys the previous week to earn the right to get trounced by the Vikings. The Purple had seventeen points on the board before Jake Plummer led Arizona to its first score. The final count was 41-21 and I was there. Thanks to that victory (and, in those days, a rare willingness to overcome my cheapness) I was also going to be there for the NFC Championship Game.

One fact that often gets overlooked when considering the NFC Championship Game that year was that the Atlanta Falcons were no slouches. They finished the season with a remarkable 14-2 record and would have been the story of the conference were it not for the Vikings. But it did not matter at the time. Vikings fans were delirious with the impending coronation of their team as champions of the NFC. And, with the way the Vikings were pummeling every team in sight, we were all convinced that it would not end with merely an NFC championship. I had even begun plotting ways to attend the big game, including trying to determine just how much money I was willing to spend for tickets. The number that I came up with would have been a lot for me at the time (and a lot for me now, for that matter), more than I could have afforded, quite frankly.

The game started amazingly slowly for two teams as blessed on the offensive side of the football as the Vikings and the Falcons that year. Atlanta scored first around the middle of the first quarter, but the Vikings answered and it was knotted at seven at the end of the first. Then the Vikings started doing what they did best that year. They put together three different scoring drives in the second quarter. The good news is that they were in the lead. The bad news was that they had only managed field goals on two of the three scoring drives.

Nonetheless, things were moving in the right direction with the Vikings ahead 20-7. Then things started to get a little ugly. Late in the half the Falcons forced a Randall Cunningham fumble deep in Vikings territory. The Falcons scored on the ensuing possession to cut the lead to 20-14.

Then the unthinkable happened. The Vikings got the ball back after the touchdown with a little less than a minute to play. People in the stands still had plenty of faith that the hometown squad could throw a few more points on the board before the half. But the Vikings did not even try. They downed the ball a couple of times to kill the rest of the half. The most prolific offense in NFL history was not even given a chance to do any additional damage by its own coaching staff. They simply gave away an opportunity to let their seven pro bowl players on offense make something happen. The people in the stands were perplexed. For the first time all season the fans felt some discontent with the team and expressed it with some boos.

Then things got worse. The highest-scoring offense in NFL history began to stall. A Falcons field goal was the only scoring in the third quarter and it cut the Vikings' lead to three. The Vikings were the first to strike in the fourth, however. A Cunningham touchdown pass to Matthew Hatchette took the lead to ten points. Atlanta answered with a field goal to bring their deficit back to seven points. But time was running out and the Vikings seemed to be picking up a little more steam.

As the clock winded down the Vikings found themselves in field goal range. With a little over two minutes left they trotted out their field goal kicker, Gary Anderson. Anderson had not only been good for Minnesota that year, he had been perfect. He made all of his kicks that season, never missing either a field goal or an extra point. Had Anderson made the field goal the three points would have pushed the lead back into two-score territory and would have effectively ended the Falcons' chances at a comeback.

But he missed. The first kicker to make all of his kicks in the regular season (and, up until that point, the postseason as well) barely missed a thirty-eight-yard try. He could not have picked a worse time for his first failed attempt.

This was the opportunity that the Falcons needed. They drove back down the field and tied the game with forty-nine seconds left. The Vikings could not muster anything with those remaining forty-nine seconds. And, they could not muster anything in overtime either. The offense that carried them all year disappeared. For a while, the two teams pushed each other around at midfield. But the Falcons were able to finally bend the Vikings defense enough to try their own thirty-eight-yard field goal deep into overtime. Morton Andersen's try was true and the dream season was dead.

Over 64,000 people attended the game that day. With the exception of three very annoying women who were wearing Falcons jerseys and were dancing and hugging each other, we all got up and began leaving without saying anything to one another. Occasionally some poor slob who had had a few too many and could not contain himself anymore would let loose with an expletive at the top of his lungs. But other than those occasional outbursts, the only other sounds were feet shuffling and jackets being zipped in preparation for a winter day that had just become much, much colder.

The only solace to be had was that Monday was a holiday and there was no work or classes scheduled. This is beneficial because I do not believe that I said a word for the next two days. I cannot be completely sure, however, because those two days are a bit foggy. The loss was so devastating that the rest of the world seemed bleary and unreal. The only truly clear memory I have from those forty-eight hours is the recurring thought that the Vikings were not going to the Super Bowl. It kept playing in my mind over and over, chipping away at my disbelief until it finally became a reality in my head. The Vikings were not going to the Super Bowl. Not after the 15-1 regular season. Not after the 556 points. Not after taking a knee to end the first half. Not after Gary Anderson's only miss of the entire year.

Life did begin again on Tuesday. But everything had changed. Nobody talked about the team anymore. The spirit of camaraderie was gone. A few folks consoled each other in the following days, but the sense of companionship was lost. It was the best year I had ever spent as a Vikings fan. But it was also, without question, the worst.

I hate the Atlanta Falcons.

NFC SOUTH

Carolina Panthers

Anticipation can be both the most exhilarating and the most nerve-wracking emotion that there is. Anticipation is all about the unexpected, and, depending on one's disposition and situation, it can be either really, really good or really, really bad.

Sometimes anticipation involves hoping and waiting and wishing. Sometimes it is about wanting the unknown to become known–particularly when you are holding hands with a first class cutie who you really like on your first date and you are scheming on how to make that first kiss a reality. Of course, there are times when you would prefer the unknown to remain unknown. For example, you might find yourself sitting outside of your boss's office. Perhaps in that moment you would prefer to remain blissfully ignorant of why the head honcho has summoned your presence. In either case, the anticipation can be overwhelming.

The anticipation before the Vikings' 2001 season was a mixture of both good and bad. On the positive side, the Vikings were coming off of a relatively successful 2000 campaign. The Vikings won the division and it was the fifth season in a row, and sixth out of the previous seven seasons, that they made it to the playoffs. The team even found its way to the NFC Championship Game for the second time in three years under Denny Green. Additionally, second-year quarterback (and first-year starter) Daunte Culpepper played exceptionally well. Daunte along with Randy Moss seemed destined to team up for tremendous success for the next ten years.

On the negative side they had gotten crushed in that NFC Championship Game. The team had blown its last three games of the year to give the number one seed away to the New York Giants and found themselves on the road for the contest. It got out of hand quickly and the Giants ended up putting a severe 41-0 beating on the Vikings. Despite consistently making the playoffs, many fans were tired of Denny Green because of his seeming inability to take the team to the Super Bowl and for other various reasons, such as some of his mind-numbingly dumb quotes to the media. The franchise's all-time leading rusher, Robert Smith, inexplicably retired in the off season while still at the peak of his career. Worst of all, offensive lineman Korey Stringer died from heat exhaustion during training camp.

Thus, the 2001 season began with plenty of both promise and questions. How would the team respond after their pitiful performance in the NFC Championship Game? Had the rapidly deteriorating defense plugged up its many holes? Could first round draft pick Michael Bennett provide the same level of production as the recently retired Robert Smith? How would the team respond to Stringer's passing? Would Denny Green be able to weather the mounting storm around him?

The first chance to answer those questions and the many more that preceded the 2001 campaign came against the Carolina Panthers. The anticipation of a new NFL season is always reason enough to get excited, but having the Panthers come to the Metrodome for the first game of the year had an additional incentive for Vikings fans to get pumped up: Todd Steussie.

Steussie was an offensive lineman and was the Vikings' first round draft pick in 1994. He had a couple of Pro Bowl years with the team, but he also became the object of derision from the fans. He developed a reputation for jumping early and getting false start penalties. That reputation was so strong that whenever the team got a false start penalty in the last three or four years of his time with the Vikings, and for three or four years after he was gone for that matter, someone in the stands would inevitably yell "STEUSSIE" in an effort to be the first to lay blame.

The 2000 season had been Steussie's last with the Vikings before moving on to the Carolina Panthers. When the 2001 schedule was announced, many fans started salivating at the prospect of making as much noise as possible in the Metrodome in that first week of the season to fluster Steussie and his new team into false start penalties. It seemed like the perfect opportunity for the fans to really help the Vikings win a game.

And thus the 2001 season began with not only the usual mix of energy and excitement of any opening day in the NFL, it also began with an exceptional amount of nervous and giddy anticipation. The Metrodome crowd was loud and was anxiously waiting to see what would happen in the new year. Between all of the past successes and failures and all of the unresolved questions and potential, the 2001 season began with an almost limitless range of possibilities.

It also began with a thud.

The Carolina Panthers received the opening kickoff of not only the game but of the year and ran it all of the way back for the touchdown. Steve Smith took it a full ninety-seven yards to the house. Seventeen seconds into the brand new NFL season and the Vikings were already losing.

Things only got worse. The supposedly unstoppable offense found absolutely no success, getting shut out in the first half. The Vikings did briefly take the lead in the third quarter on two touchdowns and a missed extra point. But the Panthers would take the lead right back and would never relinquish it again. A fourth quarter touchdown sealed it and the Panthers walked out of the Metrodome with a victory.

A season that began with a fair amount of hope (they had made the NFC Championship Game the previous year, after all) quickly began to fall apart. Denny Green was not able to hold the team together and the season just got uglier and uglier. Whereas in the prior three seasons the Vikings managed winning a double digit number of games, in 2001 they would lose eleven games. Green was let go with one game left in the regular season and the team, the media, and the fans were given a glimpse into the next four years of Mike Tice–led football. The 2001 season was a mess. The next four seasons would be a waste.

The opening day loss to the Panthers only grew worse as the season went on as well. Carolina proved to be an exceptionally bad team. Losses would pile up for the Panthers as well, and in even greater numbers for that of the Vikings. When the 2001 season came to a close, the victory that the Carolina Panthers notched against the Minnesota Vikings would be the only one of the season for the squad. The Panthers, after their glorious triumph in the Metrodome, proceeded to drop their final fifteen games of the year.

The Panthers absolutely killed all of the hopeful anticipation that came along with the beginning of the 2001 season, and they did it on the opening kickoff. The fans would not have their revenge on Todd Stuessie and the Panthers would not taste the sweetness of victory again in 2001. It lead to the downfall of Denny Green in Minnesota. In some ways, that opening day loss was the perfect way to start a season in which Mike Tice would see his first action as a head coach. Two years later Carolina was playing in a Super Bowl. Two years later Mike Tice was blowing a 6-0 start and barely missing the playoffs because his squad lost to the four teams in the NFL who tied for the league's worst record.

I hate the Carolina Panthers.

NFC SOUTH

New Orleans Saints

Mike Tice has taken his fair share of criticism in this project. From the outside one might get the impression that I have been unfair to Tice. He did manage to make the playoffs in one season, after all. It was the only year that the Vikings and the Packers met in the playoffs and Tice's crew emerged from Lambeau Field victorious. His career record of 32-33 meant, one might claim, that he was at least mediocre. Were one to make such arguments one would be wrong and extremely stupid.

The litany of examples of Tice's inability to handle the responsibilities of being the head coach of an NFL franchise are far too numerous to detail with any completeness. Instead, a small list of blunders and missteps will have to suffice. There was the Randy Ratio, the draft day fiascos (notice that the plural form of the noun is being used), the ticket scalping affair, the multiple player transgressions under his watch, and the seemingly regularly scheduled foot-in-the-mouth quote to the local media. That miniature list does not even include any of the game time silliness, such as the often crowdinduced, reactionary challenge flags, the inadequate and often counterintuitive game plans, and the inability to prepare the team for opponents, especially for those teams that the Vikings should have beaten.

Mike Tice was a bad head coach. I suppose one could make the argument that it was not his fault as he should have never been trusted with the position in the first place. Despite (or perhaps due to) a long NFL career as a player, Tice had never been a head coach at any level before he was given the Vikings job. Tice was a fairly well-respected offensive line coach, but that was about the extent of his experience before being given complete control. Red McCombs had swooped in and purchased the franchise before the '98 season. From that point forward things went downhill for the goofy Texan. His constant declarations of "Purple pride, purple pride, purple pride" never really caught on with the fan base. And by the time he hired Tice as the head coach he well into cultivating his reputation for not being willing to spend the money to produce a winning product. Tice came on the cheap and was another dart to throw at the used car salesman by those who believe that Red pinched the life out of every penny. Tice was the lowest paid head coach in the league during his entire four-year tenure and was even making less than some of the coordinators in the league.

Nonetheless, many fans were willing to give him the benefit of the doubt. Some folks were so sick of Denny Green that any change was received as a positive sign. And, back before anyone knew anything about him, Tice really did have a reputation for being an excellent offensive line coach. All of those factors, combined with the disappointing 2001 season, led many to look forward to the Tice era with a healthy dose of optimism.

The realists understood that the 2002 was also going to be a real struggle for the Vikings. They had too many holes to fill and too many questions to answer in one season. That, coupled with a rookie head coach, made it clear that the team would be spending another year on the outside looking into the playoffs. What most people with a sense of reasonableness and clarity wanted to see out of the 2002 season was the team moving in a positive and worthwhile direction.

It did not start well. The Vikings dropped their first four contests of the season. The real stinker came on a Sunday night game against the Seahawks. The Vikings looked completely overmatched and disoriented on that night in the Pacific Northwest.

However, there was some cause for optimism. With the exception of that bomb in Seattle, the team managed to keep the games close. The other three losses were all by a touchdown or less. The defense was still not very good, but the team as a whole was at least showing some heart.

And yet, there was plenty of room for pessimism as well. Tice began his career as the Vikings head man by instituting the Randy Ratio, whereby he intended that Randy Moss would be the focus of 40 percent of the team's offensive plays. Thus, Tice began his career by spelling out his game plan to the rest of the league. And while the team had managed to keep games close in those early weeks, they could not finish or find a way to win. They blew two fourth quarter leads in their first two games.

Week five brought a much needed bye for the Vikings. Despite the initial optimism, some of the more reactionary fans were losing patience with Tice and his squad. The team was able to regroup after their bye and win their first game against the Detroit Lions. From that point on, however, it was a pretty up and down stretch of games for the Vikings, with the emphasis on the down. After beating the Packers in week eleven the team went on a three-game skid to drop their record to 3-10.

Minnesota made their way to New Orleans for a week fifteen matchup with the Saints. At the time it was two teams heading in different directions. The Saints came into the game at 9-4 and on a two-game winning streak. When the contest was finished the Vikings and the Saints would continue to be two teams heading in different directions, only those directions had been radically changed.

New Orleans scored first with the field goal, but the Vikings showed a little spunk by scoring two first quarter touchdowns of their own. The Saints ended the first quarter scoring with a touchdown of their own. The teams both tallied ten points in the second quarter to give the Vikings a 24-20 first half lead.

Things began to slow down from that point on. The Saints were the only team to manage any scoring in the third quarter, with a field goal. Both teams were able to hold off the advances of the other until the Saints broke through with a little over five minutes to play in the game. The seventeen-yard touchdown pass from Aaron Brooks to Deuce McAllister gave New Orleans a five-point lead. In an effort to extend the lead to seven and to presumably prevent the Vikings from winning should they score another touchdown, the Saints went for the two-point conversion and were successful.

Down by seven the Vikings began their own march to the end zone. As time kept slipping away so did hope. The game was beginning to resemble so many others from that season, where a valiant effort would be wasted with a fourth quarter collapse. However, the Vikings were able to make their way down the field and were able to give themselves a chance to tie the game. With five seconds left to play, Daunte Culpepper found Randy Moss on a thirteen-yard touchdown pass.

Normally, such a set of circumstances would have necessitated that the Vikings kick the extra point and send the game into overtime. Had the Vikings had anything meaningful to play for by that point of the season, it is difficult to believe that even Mike Tice would have made the decision that he made on that 2002 day. But the Vikings did not have anything to play for other than pride. So Tice kept his kicker on the sideline and decided to go for two.

The two-point conversion was still a relatively new rule in the NFL at that point. And Mike Tice, for his decision that day, became the first coach in NFL history to attempt to win a game with a last-second conversion. Daunte Culpepper bull rushed his way into the end zone and the Vikings left the bayou with a one-point win.

The game was a real turning point for both squads. The

Saints went into a tailspin after the loss. They lost their final two games of the regular season for a three-game losing streak to end the year. They missed the playoffs by one game.

The Vikings, on the other hand, really turned it around. They won their next two games to finish the year with a three-game winning streak. It was of no real consequence when it came to the standings, as even with those three victories the team finished with a 6-10 record.

But it gave people hope. It gave the fans the sense that the team was finally headed in the right direction. Those three games really felt like the franchise was turning a corner. Rarely has a fan base been so happy to finish 6-10.

It also bought Mike Tice more time. Much more time, in fact, than he deserved. People were willing to look past the goof ups of the first year and give the coach the benefit of the doubt. It felt like such a growing experience that it seemed that Tice was learning from his mistakes and would not make them again.

That was hardly the case. When it was all said and done it was clear that Tice was incapable during his time with the Vikings to take the leap from an underqualified, if respected, assistant to a battle-tested and competent leader of men. The Saints contributed mightily to Tice's overly extended tenure. Had they stopped Daunte on that two-point conversion, had they not had their own history of being a collection of choking pigs, then maybe the momentum that was generated that day would have been lost and Tice would have been exposed for what he was much, much earlier. Maybe, just maybe, we all could have been spared the hideous waste of time that was the Mike Tice era of Vikings football.

I hate the New Orleans Saints.

NFC South

Tampa Bay Buccaneers

Change is an inevitable part of the human condition. However much we may want to resist it at various points in our lives, change happens. Life moves forward and we must all adapt accordingly.

This is often one of the first and one of the hardest lessons that we have to learn in life. Whether through changing schools or moving to a new city or the divorce of our parents, or all three at once, many of us learn this lesson relatively quickly. Perhaps this is one of the reasons why sports are so appealing. They generally remain relatively unchanged, or at least it seems that way in one's youth. Even when sports do change, they still manage to remain relatively stable. Players, coaches, owners, and uniforms can come and go. But, for the most part, the team is always there. In the case of football, training camp always begins near the start of August and the regular season always begins about the time that the leaves are changing colors.

Football is always there. It is reliable. It happens once a week and lasts about three hours. It can be trusted. So too, the

Tampa Bay Buccaneers could once be trusted. There used to be a time in my life when I knew that the Buccaneers would consistently provide two things, one of which was displeasing, one of which was not. But then that changed too.

From 1977 until the 2002 season the Minnesota Vikings and the Tampa Bay Buccaneers were division rivals. Yet, by most accounts, it could have hardly been considered a rivalry at all. The two teams, despite being in the same division, were nowhere close to within proximity to each other. Whereas a Vikings fan could make a relatively easy weekend road trip to see an away game against the team's other division rivals in Chicago, Detroit, and Green Bay, any journey to Tampa would have been an odyssey and could not have happened in one weekend without a plane ticket. And since the expansion Buccaneers had only been in the league since 1976, there were really not enough years to develop a thorough hatred for the squad. In fact, the most hateable thing about the Buccaneers for most Vikings fans was their orange-on-orange uniforms (which I still maintain to this very day were not that bad and would be a welcome relief in today's bland, corporate uniform culture).

And yet, in one way, they were almost the perfect division rival. Teams in the same division, of course, play each other twice a year, once at home and once on the road. By my unofficial count, the Minnesota Vikings and the Tampa Bay Buccaneers split their two annual contests for eighty-seven years in a row. It was truly ridiculous. It did not matter how pathetic the Bucs were and how good the Vikings might have been, they always seemed to split those games. Most of the time the home team would win the game. But some years they mixed it up and one squad would take a game on the road, only to drop the home contest later in the season.

The perfect example of this inevitable trend was the 1998 season. In that year the Minnesota Vikings won fifteen of the sixteen regular season contests. The one loss? To Tampa Bay. The week nine contest was held in Tampa. The Vikings had made it through the first seven games of their schedule unblemished and were finally gaining attention in the national spotlight. The Purple had a bye in week six and had played the Washington Redskins and Detroit Lions before their matchup in Florida. The combined score for the two victories against Washington and Detroit was 75-20. It is fair to state that the Vikings were on a roll heading into the game.

Also working in the Vikings favor was that they had destroyed the Buccaneers in the first week of the season by a score of 31-7. Tampa Bay would finish the '98 season at a relatively uninspiring 8-8 and were heading into their second matchup of the year with the Vikings at 3-4. Clearly Minnesota was the best team both before and after that game that year.

Alas, the Vikings were not the best team on that Sunday. The two teams traded touchdowns in the first quarter and a touchdown and a field goal in the second quarter and were tied at the half. In the second half the normally high-powered offense was held relatively in check by the Bucs. The Vikings did take a lead with touchdown in the third, which was that quarter's only score. But Tampa Bay responded in the fourth with a field goal relatively early and the game-winning touchdown with about six minutes left to play. The Vikings, who averaged almost thirty-five points a game that year, would finish with twenty-four points and only seven in the second half.

Such was the relationship between the Vikings and the Buccaneers. They seemed to always split their games. Allegedly the Vikings hold, as of the conclusion of the 2006 season, a 31-19 all-time record against the Buccaneers. But this cannot be accurate. If they have truly played fifty contests against each other, then the all-time record has to be 25-25.

That was the first thing I used to be able to count on as it concerned Tampa Bay. I knew that, regardless of the strengths of the two teams, I could mark off a win and a loss for both teams during the season. This was an especially annoying trend because of the second thing I used to be able to count on as it concerned Tampa Bay. They were always going to be bad.

I was born in 1975 and my earliest football memories begin

in the early '80s. While the Buccaneers did find a small measure of success in the very late '70s and very early '80s, I do not remember them being anything other than terrible. The Bucs made the playoffs in the strike shortened 1982 season (in which they got killed by the Dallas Cowboys 30-17) and then again in 1997. In the interim they were horrendous. In the fourteen seasons between playoff appearances, Tampa Bay's record was 64-159. For those fourteen years they would not even win 30 percent of the games they played. They were a hideous football team and could be counted on to be hideous year in and year out.

Then they started to get good. This was somewhat disconcerting, but it hardly felt all that threatening because ever since I could remember I had been conditioned to believe that Tampa Bay Buccaneers were incapable of any true success. In fact, I honestly believed that time would stop, cats and dogs would begin loving each other and having babies, and the laws of gravity would become optional before the Buccaneers would win a Super Bowl. And the dysfunctional franchise, with their terrible draft picks, idiotic free agent signings, and often downright silly head coaching hires, would never, ever, ever win a Super Bowl before the Minnesota Vikings.

But they did. The perpetually horrible team from my youth won the Super Bowl when Jon Gruden rode Tony Dungy's players all the way to the top after the 2002 season. The 2002 season, coincidentally enough, was also the first year of realignment in the NFL after the wake of the expansion. The Vikings and the Bucs, from that season forward, were in separate divisions and would no longer play each other twice a season.

It all changed. Two of the most fundamental understandings in my life as a fan were drastically altered that year. Minnesota and the Tampa Bay Buccaneers would no longer trade a win and a loss in the regular season and the really, really hideous team that I remembered from the entirety of my youth won a Super Bowl before the Vikings. After Tampa Bay's Super Bowl victory nothing felt sacred anymore.

Anything and everything could be lost to the winds of change. Except for Vikings futility. That has remained unflinchingly constant and unalterable.

I hate the Tampa Bay Buccaneers.

NFC EAST

Dallas Cowboys

Every sport has at least one team that is hated above all others. It is a team that can bring together fans of many varied franchises into a sense of unity in their displeasure for the hated team. Due to their success, their players and coaches, and their attitude, the hated team draws the ire of everyone other than their own fans (and sometimes from them as well). In baseball that team is the New York Yankees, in hockey it is the Montreal Canadiens, and in basketball it is the Boston Celtics. These teams have a rivalry with almost every other team in their respective league. In football that team is, of course, the Dallas Cowboys. For almost as many times as I have verbally tousled with a Green Bay Packers fan over our respective favorite franchises, I have commiserated with that same fan over our shared distaste for the Dallas Cowboys.

There are those who argue that a sport needs that hated team. They will claim that a sport needs a good villain who can serve in the role of the foil. It is in the best interest of the sport, they say, that the hated team be perpetually successful so that they can play the role of Goliath to other teams' David. Perhaps those people are right. Perhaps the decline in popularity of hockey and basketball can be somewhat attributed to the decline of the Canadiens and the Celtics. But I do not really care if they are right or not. I would be just as happy if the Dallas Cowboys never won another coin flip, let alone a football game, for the rest of the franchise's history.

As a Vikings fan, there are about a bijillion reasons to hate "America's Team." The Drew Pearson pushoff and the approximately forty-five whippings they gave the Purple in the '90s spring easily to mind. In fact, were one ambitious enough to take on the project, the reasons for a Vikings fan to hate the Cowboys could make for its very own book.

Of course, one reason to hate the Cowboys stands out far and above any other even in a field this crowded. That reason is so hateful that it really only needs two words the relive the suffering and the angst: the trade.

The date was October 12, 1989, and it was cause for celebration at the time. The Vikings acquired Herschel Walker in a trade from the Dallas Cowboys. The Purple, who had made the playoffs for two straight years, were looking for the last piece of the puzzle to take them over the top and into the elite of the NFL. Walker was still a hot commodity at the time. He had won the Heisman Trophy in 1982 and starred in the USFL.

Once the USFL folded Walker made his way to Dallas to play for the Cowboys. Walker had a decent first season for the Cowboys in 1986 and a nice season in the strike-shortened year of 1987, but he really broke through in 1988 when he rushed for over 1,500 yards. It looked like Walker was fulfilling his mighty promise and was becoming a true NFL superstar.

The Cowboys, on the other hand, were in a rare down period. The Tom Landry days were dying a slow, painful death and the team was scraping the bottom of the NFL barrel. In Walker's breakout year of 1988 the Cowboys would finish with a 3-13 record. The outlook was bleak for the once-proud, two-time Super Bowl champion franchise.

The crisis of the times produced the conditions for a huge shift in Dallas. Walker's breakout season would also be the last year for Landry. Jerry Jones bought the team and hired his former Arkansas teammate and University of Miami head coach Jimmy Johnson to run the squad. The Cowboys knew that they needed to completely rebuild and that Walker was their most valuable asset. The Vikings' desperation for the one player that would propel them to the Super Bowl made a trade between the two franchises seem like a natural fit.

The problem was that the Vikings gave away a good number of the players that helped them get to the playoffs in the last two years. In addition, they also gave away a good chunk of their future in the form of multiple draft picks. The tricky nature of the trade was such that it first appeared that the Cowboys would either get the players that the Vikings sent over or they would get the draft picks. In the long run, however (and I have never been able to adequately figure out how–or why–this happened), the Cowboys ended up really getting both the players and the draft picks.

When all of the dust had settled and all of the particulars had been ironed out, the Vikings basically got Herschel Walker and a small handful of mid- to low round draft picks. The Cowboys got some of the Vikings' key players, such as linebacker Jesse Solomon and cornerback Issac Holt, and a whole boatload of draft picks. Before it was all said and done the Cowboys found their way into three future Vikings' number one draft picks, three future number two picks, and a third round pick, among a few others. With that pirate treasure chest worth of draft picks the Cowboys were able to wheel and deal their way into other picks and players that they wanted. Using the generous multitude of tools they received from the Purple, Dallas was able to pick up key pieces for their future, including Russell Maryland, Darren Woodson, and a *Dancing With the Stars* champion who ended up gaining 18,355 rushing yards before his career was complete.

The 1989 season was another down year for the Cowboys, when they were only able to manage one victory to console them through their fifteen defeats. However, things turned around quickly after that. Two years after their 1-15 season, Dallas was back in the playoffs. Another season later they were Super Bowl champions yet again. It was the first of three Super Bowl championships in four years for the team that built itself upon the backs of the Vikings.

Even for all they gave up, all of the players and the draft picks and the future, it could have been worth it for the Vikings. There was still yet a way to justify the mortgaging of the franchise's future. The way it could have been worth it (or at least a lot less lopsided of a trade) was if Herschel Walker had performed as advertised.

At first it looked like he might. In his first game as a Viking he ripped up the Green Bay Packers for 137 yards and an especially memorable run in which he lost his shoe and his sock started flopping around while members of the Packers secondary tried to catch him.

But that was about it. Walker finished the year having played eleven games and with 669 yards on 169 attempts. Walker spent two more lackluster seasons with the Vikings, gaining 835 yards in 1991 for his best output with the club. In some ways, Walker was not to blame for his poor showing. The coaching staff did not give him nearly enough carries to let him get into a rhythm or to let his bruising running style wear down opponents. Nor could many athletes live up to the tremendous hype and the disturbingly large bounty that the Vikings' front office paid for him. Yet, in other ways Walker seemed plenty worthy of blame. He did not seem all that happy about the trade even though he was escaping a dire situation and landing on a playoff caliber team. He did not really acclimate himself to Minnesota, nor did he seem to even attempt to do so. He appeared to be much more interested in ballet and bobsledding. He would also occasionally put his foot in his mouth, like the time he stated something to the effect that he anticipated more success in the future because he was going to start running with his head up from then on forward. There was even one bizarre incident when he was found sleeping in his running car in a closed garage. It was never clear whether or not Walker had done this on purpose and it was a suicide attempt or if it was a bout of poor judgment that almost led to an unfortunate ending.

I refuse to make light of that particular event because whether or not it was a suicide attempt or a silly mistake, a man's life was at stake (I shall, however, continue to mock the Randy Ratio with impunity). Nonetheless, it was a clear reflection of a bad situation. The trade was unnervingly unequal from the beginning and only became more so when Walker did not play very well. In the final calculation it became clear that Walker did not want to be in Minnesota, the coaching staff did not know what to do with him when he got here, and the front office put so much faith in one player that they gave away enough of their future to build a dynasty in another city.

The Vikings were 21-22 with Herschel Walker as a member of the team. Although they made the postseason in 1989 (where they were obliterated by the San Francisco 49ers 41-13), they would miss the playoffs in the two full years he spent with the squad after that. Walker would go on to have the second of his two 1,000-yard rushing seasons in the NFL in 1992. It was the same year he left Minnesota to sign with the Philadelphia Eagles as a free agent and the same year that the resurgent Cowboys won their first Super Bowl victory under Jimmy Johnson and Jerry Jones.

I hate the Dallas Cowboys.

NFC East

New York Giants

In my formative years as both a human being and as a Vikings fan, there have been a handful of teams that have routinely been of championship caliber and, thusly, have been better than the Purple. Perhaps the most classic example is the San Francisco 49ers, who began a string of dominance whereby the NFC won fifteen of sixteen Super Bowls with their first championship at the end of the 1981 season. After the Los Angeles Raiders Super Bowl victory two years later, the team representing the NFC won the next thirteen Super Bowls. For a long time the NFC Championship Game was *the* championship game of the NFL.

The New York Giants were one of those teams to routinely make and go deep into the playoffs. The Giants of Bill Parcells won two Super Bowls mainly on the strength of a defense led by Lawrence Taylor (who, for all of the kids out there, is the reason why those of us in our thirties and above simply cannot call LaDainain Tomlinson "LT" no matter how good he is) and other notable stalwarts. Even when the AFC was able to restore some balance to the power of the conferences (and, as of late, eventually move past the NFC) the Giants were able to make it to a Super Bowl.

The Giants' third trip to the big game begins my reasoning for hating the New York Giants. It was the 2000 season and the Vikings began the year with seven consecutive wins. The 1998 season ended so heartbreakingly that it felt destined that 1999 was to be a disappointment. Although the Vikings did make the playoffs in 1999, they did not win the division and did not advance past the divisional round. With the inevitable letdown year behind the squad, the fast start to the 2000 season felt like the beginning of a big-time, bounce-back season.

The Vikings stumbled in their next two games to division foes Tampa Bay and Green Bay, but then they rattled off another four wins in a row. With about a month left in the season, the Vikings were 11-2 and had an easy track to the number one seed in the playoffs.

Then everything began to fall apart. They were throttled by the St. Louis Rams, lost to the Packers in a game that was not as close as the 33-28 final score would indicate, and got demolished by the Indianapolis Colts. The Giants, on the other hand, won their last five games of the regular season to finish at 12-4 and readily grabbed the number one seed that the Vikings had coughed up.

The teams met in the NFC Championship Game. Thanks to their late season choke job, the Vikings had to play the game on the road. It was an abysmal contest that should have been called even before the first quarter was finished. The final was 41-0 and even that monstrosity of a score did not do justice to the severe beating the Giants placed on the Vikings that day.

But that NFC Championship Game, and the Giants' general knack for being better than the Vikings during the '80s and '90s is only part of the reason why I hate them. In most respects, it should be reason enough. But New York went above and beyond the call of duty after that NFC Championship Game. They made me hate going to football games in general.

As of the conclusion of the 2006 season, the Vikings allegedly hold the edge in series history between the franchises by winning ten of the eighteen contests the two have played. But that must mean that the Vikings once held a ten-to-one or ten-to-zero edge before that NFC Championship Game. From that point forward, it seemed that the Giants began destroying the Vikings on a regular basis.

So it was when the Giants visited the Metrodome in week eight of the 2003 season. Things were going exceptionally well for the Vikings. They began the year with six straight victories and second-year head coach Mike Tice appeared to be in charge and leading his players in the right direction. I do remember having a sense of foreboding, however, as the Giants, even though they were struggling, still seemed to have Minnesota's number.

For the majority of the contest it was a tight affair. Even though the Giants came into the game having lost three straight and had a record of 2-4, they were putting up a tremendous fight. The Giants even had a three-point lead at the half. A third quarter field goal pushed the lead to six. However, the Vikings managed getting a touchdown a little over halfway through the third to take the lead by one.

Around about that time I was sitting in my obstructed view season ticket seat (it was about three rows from the top of the Metrodome, right next to a pole, provided a clear view of 90% of the field without having to lean forward (98% when leaning forward) and cost about $200 or so less than the unobstructed view seat right next to me). All of the sudden, a very drunk man fell on top of me.

I had been purchasing season tickets for about four years at that point and I had seen my fair share of drunken Metrodome patrons. I had even had some beer spilled on me on a couple of occasions. But this was the first time that another human being had landed upon me.

It was clear that the man was no longer in a state where he could sit by himself unattended, let alone watch or comprehend the game. I pushed him back into his proper row above me and began asking my friend who was at the game with me to call down the aisle to get an usher. I was under the impression that it was possible that the man had hurt himself in the fall, and even if he had not hurt himself in the fall, he was dangerously drunk and had become a threat to himself and those like me who were sitting in front of him. My friend responded quickly and began telling other folks in the row to begin calling for an usher or medical attention.

It was at this time that a ball of human flesh stood up and began vehemently declaring that no usher was needed. I can only say with uncertain confidence that the ball of flesh was a woman because whatever feminine quality or charm this person may have held at one time was buried deeply under mounds of grotesque fat and a reddened face that belied its own share of alcohol consumption that Sunday morning and afternoon.

I could not quite tell what was happening right away because my first concern was making sure the drunken man got the medical attention he probably needed. Of course, it did not help my cognitive abilities that my second concern was keeping an eye on the game while play continued and my third concern was hoping that the usher would haul the guy away so that I could watch the rest of the game in relative peace. Nonetheless, the clues kept adding up until I finally got it. The final piece of the puzzle for me was when I saw the ball-woman scream for the third or fourth time "We don't want an usher!"

I absolutely could not believe it. The rotund banshee was attempting to turn away aid and/or medical attention that might have been vitally necessary. It was more important to this asinine creature who was as wide as she (?) was tall to watch the rest of the game than it was to attend to the potential injuries or alcohol poisoning of the unfortunate, drunken soul who was somehow connected to her/it.

Despite the ball-woman's protestations against it, an usher and a cop did finally make their way to the top of the Metrodome. Somehow, the drunken lout who had fallen on me had woken up just enough from his stupor to feign a sense of coherence. Between the drunk's charade and the flesh banshee's insistence, the two of them were able to convince the proper authorities that they were fine and should be allowed to stay at the game.

Meanwhile, as this whole ridiculous mess was going on, the game took a drastic turn for the worse. Momentum seemed to immediately shift to the Giants after the alcoholic fan had tumbled forward and onto my back. The Giants took charge of the game, scored thirteen points in the fourth quarter, easily stymied all efforts by the Vikings, and cruised the rest of the way for an easy victory. Vikings owner Red McCombs, who was already well into the early stages of turning himself into a local villain, apparently left his perspective in the owners box of the stadium as he went into the locker room and ripped his "embarrassing" players for the loss.

The Vikings, despite Red's assessment, were hardly in a terrible position after the loss dropped their record to 6-1. Yet, the rest of the season would turn out to be a mess. The Giants were just the first of the four teams with the worst record in the NFL to hang a loss on the Vikings. The Raiders, Chargers, and, most painfully, Cardinals would also finish 2003 at 4-12 and would also defeat the Vikings that season. Minnesota would miss the playoffs by one game that year. Had they beaten those four teams with the worst record in the league, they would have finished at 13-3 and would have had the number one seed in the playoffs.

It should be noted that, in doing research for this project, I came to find out that the Giants did not actually dominate the Vikings in the manner that I had previously believed. In fact, the two teams have played each other pretty evenly ever since that 41-0 NFC Championship Game.

Nonetheless, it should still be understood as a testament to the power of both that NFC Championship Game and having the drunk fall on me that I felt the way that I did before I looked up the records. The NFC Championship Game produced such a sense of dread that I must have automatically assumed that, from that point forward, the Giants owned the Vikings. And the drunk and the female parade float were not only so annoying that I began hating to go to Vikings games, their selfish actions turned the game completely around and sealed it for the Giants.

No wonder I believed that the Giants thoroughly dominated the Vikings for a stretch of four or five years. I had it beaten into me over the head by a drunk man's body. You would feel the exact same way under those circumstances.

I hate the New York Giants.

NFC East

Philadelphia Eagles

In his four years and one game as head coach for the Minnesota Vikings, Mike Tice earned a career record of 32-33. His career playoff winning percentage was slightly better than that of his regular season winning percentage thanks to one victory and one loss. Both of those postseason games occurred in the 2004 playoff season.

The numbers in and of themselves do not seem to be all that bad. They are certainly not terrific, as Tice ultimately did not win as many games as he lost as a head coach. But, on first glance, they do not seem worthy of the (well-deserved) shellacking I have given Tice throughout the course of this project. According to the numbers, Tice was mediocre–nothing more, nothing worse.

Yet, as the old adage goes, statistics are like bikinis: they show you quite a bit, but not the stuff you really want to see. The fiasco that was Tice and the Vikings' 2003 season has been well chronicled in this project. Suffice it to say that it really was the most Viking of all of the Vikings seasons. In the long run, the almost even career record is very misleading.

In fact, the Mike Tice regime can probably be best summed up in one play. That one play occurred not in the quintessential Vikings season of 2003, but in a 2004 playoff loss in Tice's lone opportunity in the postseason as a head coach. The opponent on the fateful day of that play, the Philadelphia Eagles, had their own recent history of troubled times and are probably the least hateful of the teams in the NFC East. Nonetheless, they are still hateful for how they exposed Tice and the '04 team for the frauds that they were (and they got what they deserved for trading for the petulant crybaby, team wrecker Terrell Owens).

The 2004 season actually resembled 2003 in many ways. Like in '03, the Vikings got off to a quick start in '04 by beginning the year 5-1 and showing promise. However, again like in '03, that promise was fairly quickly squelched. A stretch of games with the New York Giants, Indianapolis Colts, and Green Bay Packers quickly turned a happy and shiny 5-1 record into a dull and uninspiring 6-4 record. The rest of the regular season more or less followed in the same vein. A couple of wins would be followed by a couple of losses and so on and so forth. There was one last opportunity for the Vikings to improve their lot in life when they beat the Detroit Lions in week fifteen. But two consecutive losses to the Packers and the Washington Redskins to close the season left Minnesota with an 8-8 record and a bad taste in the mouths of the team and the fans. The situation was in no way improved at the end of the Washington game when Randy Moss decided to leave the field early while his team still had a chance, even as remote and improbable as it was, to tie or win the game.

Luckily for the Vikings, the NFC was at its lowest point in at least twenty-five years. Minnesota's unimpressive 8-8 record was still good enough to qualify the team for that season's playoffs. Randy Moss took a lot of heat both locally and nationally for deserting his teammates in the waning seconds of the game against Washington. However, he would have a chance to make amends in the postseason.

The Vikings' opponent for their wildcard playoff matchup was none other than the Green Bay Packers. It was the first time that the longtime division foes would meet in the postseason and there was reason for pessimism as a Vikings fan. In both of the regular season contests that year, the Packers managed pulling out victories with last-second field goals. It felt like Green Bay had Minnesota's number that season and it would have been unbearable to have to suffer a third defeat to the Cheeseheads that season.

But then something magical happened. Minnesota scored their first touchdown in under two minutes and threw seventeen points on the scoreboard before the Packers managed their first field goal. The game was never really all that close as the Vikings cruised to a 31-17 victory. The highest of all the highlights of the day might just have been when Randy Moss, who obviously had absolutely no concern for his public image at this point, pantomimed mooning the Lambeau Field crowd. Apparently the good folks of Green Bay had cultivated a long tradition of welcoming the opposing team's bus to the stadium with a salute of their bare (and, one must assume, pasty and gigantic) bottoms and Randy was just giving a little back to the community. The gesture sent the game's television announcer, Joe Buck, into a self-righteous seizure (although, to be fair, it has been suggested that Buck and others believed that Randy was pantomiming dropping something more than just his trousers).

The victory over the Packers earned Minnesota the right to travel to Philadelphia to take on the number one seeded Eagles. In the immediate wake of the victory in Green Bay, there were a lot of Vikings fans (myself included) who were just happy to see the team beat the Packers in the playoffs. All of the rest of what was to come would be gravy. But as the contest against the Eagles approached, a lot of Vikings fans (myself included) believed that, if the team gave a strong enough effort, as they had against the Cheeseheads, the Vikings just might be able to sneak out of Philly with another upset.

We were wrong. Or, to be precise, we never really got to see if we might be right. As well as the Vikings played the previous week in Green Bay, they would perform just as awfully in Philadelphia. There was a whole range of Vikings miscues. The ground game never got off the ground. Daunte Culpepper threw two third quarter interceptions while the team was still clinging to life. Especially notable was the sequence after the Vikings scored their first touchdown.

By that point, the Eagles has scored two touchdowns within the first sixteen minutes of the game clock to take a 14-0 lead. Momentum was clearly on the Eagles' side, but Minnesota was able to put a drive together after Philly's second touchdown and they scored about five minutes into the second quarter. Perhaps, I thought to myself as I watched the game, momentum was swinging back in favor of the Vikings.

Nope. The Eagles took the opening kickoff forty-eight yards to the Vikings' forty-six yard line. A couple of stupid Vikings penalties for thirty-three yards later and the Eagles were in the red zone. A couple of plays later, Philly quarterback Donovan McNabb found tight end L.J. Smith for a pass. Smith caught the ball but then fumbled. This potential lucky break for the Vikings very quickly turned sour when Philly wide receiver Freddie Mitchell recovered the ball in the end zone. The whole despicable affair took twenty-nine seconds off of the game clock. Less than half of a minute of game time after the Vikings scored their first touchdown of the game, the Eagles grabbed a hold of the momentum once again and would not relinquish it for the rest of the afternoon.

And yet, despite the ridiculousness of this series of plays, it is not the sequence that defined the Mike Tice era. That inglorious distinction belongs to a play that would come later in the second quarter.

Even after Philly regained a two-touchdown lead after the fumble in the end zone, the Vikings were able to muster a little bit of gumption and make another drive deep into Eagle territory. A touchdown would have shown the heart and determination that was so desperately lacking in the Tice era. Alas, the Vikings were stymied and lined up for a field goal.

At the time, I was living in the twin cities. A local, independent movie theater near my apartment had an absolutely wonderful promotion where they would show local games of importance on their movie screen. Admission was free and the snack bar was open for business. There was even a guy who sold hot dogs in the lobby.

It was, by far, the best local sports promotion I had ever heard of or participated in. The idea was just tremendous because it combined the best of both worlds. You got the sense of community and connectedness that goes along with attending a live game. But you also got all of the replays and extra angles that a game on television provides. Additionally, the movie house had a ton of seats and there was generally enough space to spread out without having to be shoulder-to-shoulder with your fellow fans.

There was a feeling in the building before the game that the Vikings might be able to pull off the upset. That feeling quickly dissipated. By the time the Vikings lined up for the field goal, people were actively advocating for a fake field goal to turn things around.

Unfortunately, Mike Tice often coached as if he were an impassioned fan and not a more levelheaded, knowledgeable, experienced coach. For example, Tice apparently did not understand that the challenge rule for coaches was discretionary and that it was possible to go through an entire football game without throwing the red flag on the field.

So, Tice attempted the fake field goal. The plan was to take advantage of Randy Moss's reputation for lackadaisical effort. Randy was supposed to stroll toward the sideline in feigned contempt and disgust, but not to leave the field before the ball was snapped. Then, when the ball was snapped, Randy was supposed to rush toward the end zone and backup quarterback and field goal holder Gus Frerotte was supposed to find the presumably wide open Moss for the touchdown.

There were a lot of suppositions and presumptions built into the play. Too many, apparently, for Tice and his staff to handle.

Word of the fake did not get out to everybody who needed to know and the Vikings lined up with the full eleven men of the special teams unit on the field. Moss, recognizing that he was the twelfth man on the field and would have drawn a penalty, did the only thing that he could and hustled to the sidelines. With the only option that had been drawn up standing on the sidelines, Frerotte was hung out to dry and the whole play collapsed upon itself.

After the game, Tice had the audacity to state that the fake field goal had been "perfectly designed." But in reality it was a microcosm of his coaching career. The play was much too complicated for Tice and his staff to pull off. Nor, apparently, had anyone considered inserting a second option for Frerotte and the team if the first option was unavailable (which it obviously was). It killed any momentum for the Vikings from that point forward. And, instead of admitting that it was a horrendous mistake, Tice again made himself out to be a donkey's rear in the local media with a silly quote. Therein lies the Mike Tice era in a nutshell.

The Eagles were a good team and probably would have won the game in any event. But they were also the recipient of a boatload of boneheaded Vikings' mistakes. And, in the end, they found a way to perfectly sum up the four plus years of Mike Tice football.

I hate the Philadelphia Eagles.

NFC East

Washington Redskins

I desperately hate this team for two very different reasons. The first reason should be obvious, but apparently it is not.

I have a question to which I have never been able to find an adequate answer. Let us imagine a normal person living in the Washington D.C. area. Let us also imagine that this person is the kind of human being who would never dream of saying the "n-word." And this person also cringes, and maybe even says something, when she or he hears another make a joke or comment about "all of those immigrants" who are "taking our jobs." Nor does this person condone it when a friend, family member, or coworker squints her or his eyes and spews forth a bunch of sounds meant to derisively ape an Asian language.

It is not too hard to imagine this person. In fact, our hypothetical Washington D.C. resident, and that person's rejection of clearly bigoted words and actions, is someone to whom we can aspire to be.

So how is it that our supposedly non-racist Washingtonian

can be comfortable with painting his or her face, wearing a headdress of dyed chicken feathers, and engaging in behavior that mocks Native American heritage and beliefs at a Redskins game? How can a word like "Redskin," which is, unquestionably, a slur, still be amongst the popular vernacular? Equally as baffling, how can this be a nickname for a team in the nation's capital? The very center of the American government continues to embrace what is, easily, the most derogatory sports team name in the United States? What does that say about our country?

It does not matter where you stand on the Native American mascot issue. You may be one who thinks they should all be banned, or you may think that it is an example of political correctness run amok (and if you think this, you are stupid). But you cannot deny that a name like "Redskins" is just plain bad.

I am of Native American heritage. But even if I was not of that background, I could not possibly imagine thinking this team name was, in any way, right or appropriate. I could continue about "Indian mascots" ad naseum. The subject is worthy of its own book (and, in fact, a few good ones have been written). However, I will spare you a more complete diatribe. Suffice it to say that I have yet to hear one reasonable justification for retaining any Indian mascot, let alone the Redskins.

Were its racist team name the only reason why I hate Washington D.C.'s football team it would be more than enough. However, there is another reason why I hate them. They made me suffer through the worst game I have ever watched in my life and every game thereafter.

I had turned twelve not too long before the playoffs for the 1987 season started and I was at a crossroad in my life as a Vikings fan. The Vikings had a good team that year and it would be the first of three consecutive seasons that they would make the playoffs. However, it was also a year of labor strife, with the players going on strike in the middle of the season.

Even though I was still very much a young man at the time,

I knew well enough that the situation was disgusting. While I was unaware of the particulars surrounding the strike, I was able to ascertain that greedy owners did not want to give more money to greedy players, and the resultant consequence was one of the rare times that I was not able to count on seeing my favorite team every fall Sunday.

The situation only became worse when the owners decided to continue playing games (and charging for tickets) with replacement players. The scrubs played three games before the actual NFL players returned to the game. In a fit of absolute ridiculousness, the NFL decided that the games with the replacement players would count against the schedule.

The Vikings did have a good team that year. In fact, they started the season with two victories before the players went on strike. However, the replacements that the Vikings obtained for those shameful three weeks were horrible. That situation, coupled with the fact that Jerry Burns seemed thoroughly uninterested in coaching the scrubs, led to three ugly losses. As talented as the real 1987 Vikings were, they ultimately finished with an 8-7 record. Luckily, that mediocre showing was just enough to get them into the playoffs.

Having just turned twelve, and having watched every game of that tremendously frustrating season (including the games with the replacement players), I was convinced that the Vikings were going to get destroyed in the playoffs. In fact, I was so sure of that outcome that I did not want to watch the wildcard game against the New Orleans Saints. I also knew that, even at that early age, I was fed up with the frustration and ridiculousness that came along with being a Vikings fan. I was ready to give up on the team and I was looking for that one last loss in a crummy season to set me free.

A loss against the Saints would have done it. Had the Vikings had enough decency to lose to New Orleans, I truly believe that I would have been so fed up with the team that I might never have watched them again. I was twelve after all, and still in a position to find new interests that were less painful.

But they did not lose. In fact, they crushed the Saints. After giving up the first touchdown of the game, the Vikings scored the next twenty-four points to roll to a 44-10 victory. Nonetheless, it did not really matter to my twelve-year-old mind. The next opponent, the San Francisco 49ers, were far superior to New Orleans and would not fail as the Saints had failed.

But a funny thing happened. The Vikings not only beat the Niners, they did so in convincing fashion. Anthony Carter set an NFL playoff record with 227 receiving yards for the game and the team as a whole had a 20-3 lead at the half. San Francisco scored three touchdowns in the second half, but the Vikings kept pace well enough with sixteen second-half points of their own. When the dust settled, Minnesota walked out of the bay area with a 36-24 win.

Another funny thing happened. The twelve-year-old version of me began believing in the Vikings again. Whereas I had been ready to write them off for the rest of my life two weeks earlier, after they beat the 49ers to reach the NFC Championship Game I had to concede that they could go all the way. With all of my youthful exuberance I jumped back on the bandwagon as quickly and decisively as I could. The frustration of the regular season had melted away, only to be replaced with a young man's hope. My Vikings were one game away from the Super Bowl.

I had been a reluctant viewer of the playoff games against New Orleans and San Francisco. But I could not wait for the NFC Championship Game against the Redskins. I was at my grandparents' house and I was prepared to celebrate a victory.

Were I an impartial observer I might have appreciated the ferocious battle that was that game. It was a defensive contest, with both teams' defense generally knocking around the other teams' offense. But I was not an impartial observer, and the entire game was a struggle. The Redskins scored in the first quarter and the Vikings were not able to tie the game until fairly late into the second quarter. The same thing happened to start the second half as well. The

Redskins got a field goal and it seemed to take forever for the Vikings to get one of their own. Not long thereafter the Redskins got another touchdown to make the game 17-10.

As the game waned, the Vikings made one final push to the end zone. I was sitting on the edge of my grandparents' couch as the Vikings were finally moving the ball. That final drive made it all the way down to Redskins' six yard line, but stalled from there. The last gasp died an especially ghastly death when Darrin Nelson dropped a pass on fourth down. Nelson may not have gotten into the end zone on the play, but he would have at least had a first down and given the team another couple of chances to punch the ball into the end zone.

As soon as that pass slipped through Nelson's hands, Redskins players began jumping up and down in celebration. The loss was so traumatic that a friend who I would meet later in life, and who was old enough to have seen the Super Bowl losses, would have a clear memory of being in stands in the corner of the building where Nelson dropped the ball. He once vividly described to me the exact angle from which he saw the play. The only problem was that the game was played in Washington D.C. and my friend has never been to RFK Stadium. The blunt force of the loss was so devastating that it caused him to have memories of experiences he has never had.

As for myself, when the pass slipped through Nelson's hands, I fell off of my grandparents' couch and onto the floor. I dropped to my hands and knees and buried my head between my arms. I stayed that way for about ten minutes trying to keep myself from crying. I wanted to keep my composure so that no one would see that I was so close to tears and so they could not tease me. Lying there on the floor was the only way I could figure out how to keep myself together.

In retrospect, however, I wish that someone would have seen that I was on the verge of weeping uncontrollably. I wish someone had seen it and I wish they had teased me so unmercifully that I never wanted to watch another football game ever again. That way I could have let go. That way I could have found something different to fill my time and I would have saved myself another two decades or so of the misery that is being a Vikings fan. That way I would have never been compelled to write this book when I should have been doing so many more things that could benefit me and my family. That way I would be free.

I hate the Washington Redskins.

NFC North

Chicago Bears

Much like the United Nations has permanent members and temporary members on its security council, I have permanent members and temporary members of my top three hated football teams in the NFL. The third spot in the triumvirate is generally up for grabs, with the leading contenders at any given time being teams like the Dallas Cowboys, San Francisco 49ers, and Washington Redskins. But there are two permanent members: the Green Bay Packers and the Chicago Bears.

I cannot imagine a world in which I do not hate these two teams. But that is in the here and now. I must confess that I did not used to hate the Packers nearly as much as I should have when I was growing up. The Packers of the 1980s and early '90s were generally terrible and not much of the threat. From 1980 to 1994 the best record the Cheeseheads could muster was 9-7.

When I moved to the twin cites in the mid-'90s and began attending the University of Minnesota (which is practically overrun with Wisconsinites in desperate search of the good education they are unable to find in their home state), I truly learned to hate the Packers with the verve and tenacity that is befitting of that franchise. But until that point, the team that I hated the most was the Chicago Bears.

For the bulk of the franchise's history, especially in the post–George Halas years, the Chicago Bears have also been generally terrible. Unfortunately, one of their few bright spots as a team came at about the time I started really getting into football. Mike Ditka, Jim McMahon, Walter Payton, and, more than any other, Refrigerator Perry, were the bane of my existence.

The whole collection of Bears teams from that era routinely kicked the stuffing out of the Vikings. It was one of the first examples in my early life that there were always going to be teams that were better than the Vikings and I hated the Bears for it. Those teams from that era are also hateful for inflicting the "Super Bowl Shuffle" upon the world. I would rather scrape my ears out with a rabid porcupine than ever listen to that hideous piece of trash ever again. Music has meant less to humanity ever since that so-called song was released.

As you might be able to imagine, I could list an untold number of offenses that the Bears have perpetrated against the Vikings. Yet, one stands out above the rest. One game, more than any other, pops inside my head when I think about how much I hate the Chicago Bears.

That game was not Chicago's Super Bowl victory. Nor did it occur in the '80s when the Bears routinely mauled the Vikings (please note that I recognize the bad pun that I just used; it is reflective of how terrible it was to watch those games). Rather, it occurred at the very tail end of the run put together by those Bears teams.

In the holiday season of late 1994 and early 1995 I was still living in my hometown of Grand Forks, North Dakota. I was in the midst of the one year I would not attend school between high school and college. Instead of pursuing education, I was pursuing lung cancer by working in a local bingo hall. The only thing that the old ladies who routinely played liked more than bingo was their cigarettes (a close second was leering at and snickering over a young author who happened to be working there at the time). I have never been a smoker. In fact, I have never lit up and taken a puff of a cigarette in my life, but in the span of a shift at the bingo hall I have no doubt that I went through a whole carton of them.

That whole year was aimless and a gigantic waste of time. The money was nowhere worth all of the carcinogenic inhalation. I was stuck in a dispiriting cycle of staying up late (with nothing to do), finally getting to sleep, getting up in just enough time to go to work, getting off from work anywhere between 10:30 p.m. and 1:30 a.m., and doing it all over again. I was also living in a horrible little efficiency apartment where, due to the size of my furniture, I had to sleep in the kitchen. I do not remember that year with any particular fondness.

There was one bright spot, however. The Vikings won the division and were playing well in Denny Green's third year as head coach. It was even more impressive considering the depth of their competition. Back in those days there were three divisions and three wildcard teams. That particular season, all three wild cards, Chicago, Green Bay, and the Detroit Lions, came from the same division as the Vikings.

As was mandated back in those days, the division winner with the worst record had to play in the wild card weekend. The Vikings were that team in 1994 and it felt a little unfair. It did not seem like they should be penalized because they had won the toughest division in football that season. Nonetheless, the Vikings were the division champs and would be hosting the Chicago Bears on January 1, 1995. It was a little troubling that starting quarterback Warren Moon was injured, but the word was that he would be playing that Sunday.

A good friend of mine, who was living in the twin cities at the time, was back home for the holidays. He and I walked into a local music store and ticket outlet early in that week and were shocked to find out that tickets to the playoff game were still available (we were still fairly young and naïve at the time). We spent a little bit of time comparing schedules and scheming, and finally came to the conclusion that we could go to the game. He did not have a car back then and needed a ride back to Minneapolis anyway. So, despite the fact that they were a little too pricey for a bingo hall employee's salary, we bought tickets.

Even though we figured out that we could go to the game, it was going to be a tight fit. Grand Forks is about four and a half to five hours of driving time from the twin cities and I had to work at the bingo hall until 1:00 a.m. or so on New Year's Eve into New Year's Day. We would not even get a chance to hit the road until 2:00 a.m. at the earliest. On top of which I had to be back to Grand Forks on the 2nd for work.

Nonetheless, we had bought the tickets and were determined to make it to the game. We decided to get some food at a twenty-four-hour breakfast place before we started our trip. At said establishment we, as you might expect, ran into plenty of drunks who decided their first meal of the new year had to be pancakes. One such gentleman came up to the booth where my friend and I were sitting and asked me what my major was. I politely explained that I was not in school, but the drunk would not accept that for an answer. He was convinced that he had seen me on campus. He did not leave until I told him I was majoring in something or other. At first he stated that the people in my made-up major were arrogant, but I assured him that I was not like that and he finally went away.

With that omen hanging over us, we hit the interstate. It was snowing the entire way and it probably took longer than it should have taken. Regardless, we got to the cities with plenty of time to get at least a little rest. After a couple of hours of sleep we had another, much less eventful meal and made our way to the game.

It was the first NFL game I had ever seen live. When I walked into the stadium I was struck by just how bright the goalposts were. For whatever reason, that first thought as I looked out at the Metrodome turf has always stuck with me. In any event, the game started out well. The Vikings were the first team to score and carried a 3-0 lead into the second quarter. Two other gentlemen who were about the same age as my friend and me would run up and down the stairs of the stadium high-fiving everyone after a good play. Soon, we were joining them.

It only got worse from that point on, however. Warren Moon really was injured and probably should not have been playing in that game. The Bears used a quick count to keep the Vikings defense off their guard and scored two touchdowns in the second quarter. It was never close from that point forward and the Bears steamrolled the Vikings for a 35-18 victory. The Metrodome deflated pretty quickly. It was not too long before the high-fiving gentlemen were no longer wasting their energy rushing up and down the stairs.

The mood walking out of the stadium was ugly. That ugliness carried throughout the rest of my trip to the twin cities. My friend and I could talk about nothing other than the disgusting whipping we had just seen. When I left the cities in the cold and the snow and the emptiness in the wake of the holiday season, I was infuriated. The whole trip home all I could do was calculate the number of hours I had to work at the cancer-causing bingo hall to make the money to buy the tickets and the gas and pay for the food that I had consumed on the trip. Suffice it to say that multiple work days were involved.

I have seen the Bears beat the Vikings on a number of occasions. I have even watched the Bears beat the Vikings in Chicago on one occasion. Bears fans were not particularly sympathetic as my friends and I walked back to the car after that one. But for all of the losses over all of the years, that playoff defeat on the first day of 1995 when I was a poor, unhappy bingo hall worker was the worst of them all.

I hate the Chicago Bears.

NFC NORTH

Detroit Lions

Is it possible to hate something because you do not hate it?

For as long as the Minnesota Vikings have been playing football in the NFL they have been in the same division as the Detroit Lions. Coincidentally, as long as the Minnesota Vikings have been playing football in the NFL they have been in the same division with the Chicago Bears and the Green Bay Packers.

In the case of the latter teams, familiarity has bred contempt. Talk to any Vikings fan and she or he will impassionedly tell you about her or his dislike for the Bears and the Packers. They will recount games and plays and moments when the either the Chicago or Green Bay franchise gave it to the Vikings in a bad way, or conversely they will tell you about the games, plays, and moments when Minnesota delivered a crushing blow from the hammer of defeat straight to the faces of the Bears or the Packers. With either Chicago or Green Bay, the rivalry feels historic. There is a sense of gravitas and purpose. A fan of any of the three squads knows full well that a game against the other two teams has meaning.

Games against the Detroit Lions? Not so much. Games against the Lions come and they go. Generally they result in victories for the Vikings. Yet, even when they result in losses, it is more irritating than it is soul crushing. A loss to the Packers can ruin a whole month if not a whole season. The same can be said about the Bears. A loss to the Lions never lingers anywhere close to that long.

In fact, games between the Vikings and the Lions are rarely all that memorable. There are a few exceptions. In 1995 the Vikings played the Lions on Thanksgiving Day. The game was an absolute shootout with the two teams combining for eighty-two points. Minnesota scored four touchdowns in the first half, including a punt return and a fumble return for scores in the second quarter. However, the Vikings were held relatively in check in the second half, mustering only ten points. The Lions, on the other hand, scored twenty second-half points and won the game by a final score of 44-38. Warren Moon had an excellent day for the Purple throwing for 384 yards and three touchdowns. But he was bested by Scott Mitchell and his 410 passing yards and four touchdowns.

Another somewhat memorable game occurred in November of 2000 when the Vikings hosted the Lions in the Metrodome. There was a sense of anticipation in the stadium that day because Cris Carter was almost assuredly going to make his 1000th catch of his career that afternoon. Minnesota took an early lead in the game, scoring a touchdown about halfway through the first for that quarter's only points. However, a drive near the end of the first quarter left everyone with bated breath. Carter was at career catch 999 with the Vikings on the Lions' four yard line. The first play of the second quarter went to Carter in the back of a corner of the end zone for the milestone. The crowd, the team, and Carter celebrated. Then, as one might expect, the natural deflation after such a monumental achievement occurred. The Vikings got another field goal before the half and then did not score again until late in the fourth quarter. Luckily, the Lions were not that good and could do little to capitalize on the Vikings' apathy. The Lions did pull it to within a touchdown early in the fourth, but that was as close as it got. Another really late touchdown made the final score of 24-17 seem a little more respectable then the game actually was.

So, that is about it for games that easily jump to one's memory. Part of the reason that it has not been much of a rivalry is that the Lions have been perpetually mediocre to bad. During the course of my lifetime Detroit has only won three division titles. And one of those division titles, the one in 1983, should not even really count because the Lions, with a marginal 9-7 record, only managed not to flounder as much as the rest of the division. They were briefly decent in the 1990s when Barry Sanders was running wild for them (Sanders, by the way, was so good that he is the only non-Vikings player whose jersey I have ever seriously considered purchasing). The other two Lions' division titles of my lifetime, in 1991 and 1993, were legitimate because of Sanders. But then he unexpectedly retired and Detroit became bad again. Then they decided they no longer wanted to compete at an NFL level so they hired Matt Millen and have held on to him for far too many years.

Detroit is also annoying because they routinely ruin what should otherwise be a perfectly reasonable Thanksgiving Day. Thanksgiving is generally my favorite holiday of the year. It lacks the stress of having to buy presents, but it provides the food in mass quantities. Additionally, as someone who has never been asked to cook something for the holiday, it is particularly stress-free for me. Of course, each year I also convince myself that another benefit to Thanksgiving is the football.

And every year I am wrong. The beauty about football on Sundays is that if the game you are watching is bad, there is often another game on a different channel. If that game is bad, the network broadcasting the bad game will usually switch to a much better contest. This is obviously not so on Thanksgiving. Your choices are the Dallas game (and anybody who is not ready to throw up their Thanksgiving meal when watching those pigs is un-American) and the Detroit game. The Detroit alternative used to not be so bad when Sanders was around to liven things up. But now it is generally a glorified scrimmage for the Lions' opponent. Detroit, with the state they are currently in and have generally been in for decades now, actually makes the Thanksgiving Day football detract from the holiday.

Even so, that is not enough reason to hate them. The bad football generally provides a person with an opportunity to take a desperately needed nap anyway. Thus, the Lions are not really hateable for their desecration of the Thanksgiving Day holiday. And they are not hateable for any particular slight perpetrated upon the Vikings. Why, then, are they hateable?

They are hateable because they are not hateable. They are just the Lions. They pose no real threat and they never really bother anyone. This makes for the most tepid and lame division "rivalry" in the history of humankind. Twice a year a Vikings fan is subjected to having to deal with these chumps. And twice a year it really is not all that fun. If the Vikings win, then so what? They should beat the Lions. And if they lose, then so what? The Lions will find a way to drop the next three or four in a row to Minnesota.

I know Bears fans and I know Packers fans. It is not only possible to get riled up and start good-natured arguments with them, it is expected and encouraged. But I do not know any Lions fans. In fact, I am not sure that they exist. They are not a rival. But the Vikings have to play them twice a year anyway. They are, by far, my least favorite games of the year.

I hate the Detroit Lions.

NFC NORTH

Green Bay Packers

There are so many reasons to hate the Green Bay Packers. So very, very many reasons.

The easiest way to go about writing this section would be to make fun of Packers fans. They are a disturbingly unique lot, after all. Maybe it comes from living in Wisconsin, which is a weird, goofy place (for both better and worse). Maybe it comes from identifying with beer and cheese. When your cultural identity revolves around the products of fermentation, it probably is only a matter of time before your mind goes a little sour as well. Or maybe it is because they are a part of a cult. The whole "community ownership" of the franchise is not so much a socialist success as it is a scary collectivity of hierarchical members who do the bidding of the higher-ups. Or maybe it is because when you live in Green Bay, and you have absolutely nothing else going for you, it becomes easy to obsess and identify with the team at an unhealthy level.

But I do not want to take the easy way out on this section. I do not want to make fun of Packers fans. Truth be told, I generally like the Packers fans that I know. They remind me of the type of dumb dog you might have owned when you were a kid. They are loyal, obedient, generally good-natured (as long as you do not try to take away their food or give them too much beer), and aware of their place in life. Sometimes they want too much attention, but if you whack them on the nose with a newspaper, it seems to calm them down.

Thus, I will not make fun of Packers fans. Rather, I want to discuss another of the multitude of reasons why I hate the Packers: Brett Favre.

Let us get one thing straight before we delve too deeply into why Brett Favre is the most worthy reason to discuss why I hate the Green Bay Packers. I do not hate him for the reasons you might think, or for the reasons most Vikings fans hate him. In fact, there was a time about half a dozen years or so ago when I was willing to declare Brett Favre unhateable.

You see, I believe that it is possible for an athlete to be so gifted and so talented and so accomplished that they reach a level where you can no longer hate that athlete. You might still despise the team for whom the elite athlete plays. You can most certainly still hate the outcome that the elite athlete perpetuates upon your team. But you can no longer hate the athlete.

The pantheon of unhateable athletes is small, but easily recognizable. Barry Sanders played at a level where he became unhateable (although it may have helped that he generally played for very poor teams). I think Joe Montana falls into this category as well. So does Lawrence Taylor.

Undoubtedly the greatest example of the unahateable athlete of recent memory is Michael Jordan. By the end of his run in Chicago it was easy to be sick of the Bulls. And everybody outside of Illinois was happy that they basically blew up in the wake of the '97-'98 season. Even so, you could not hate Michael Jordan. He was just too good. Even if you did not like the outcomes that his talent produced, you had to give him the respect he deserved for accomplishing what he did.

Again, about a half a dozen years or so ago I was willing to put Brett Favre in this category. Although I desperately hated that the brought a Super Bowl to Green Bay and he put more than a few good whippings on the Vikings I could not deny his greatness. He was an exceptional quarterback who, by his very presence, made Green Bay a threat to win it all every year.

However, the pantheon of unhateable athletes has some very strict entrance requirements and by-laws. And getting into that exclusive club does not guarantee you a lifetime membership. The smart elite athletes (like Sanders and Jim Brown) retire while they are part of the group. The not-so-bright ones risk their membership by hanging on well past their prime. Although the six championships would seem to assure his place among the elite, Michael Jordan risked his status with his ill-fated comeback with the Washington Wizards. Had Montana flamed out with Kansas City, instead of bringing them to an AFC Championship Game, he might have put himself in jeopardy as well.

And so it is with Brett Favre. He once was on the verge of kicking in the door to the unhateable athlete club and forcing his way inside. In fact, had he retired half a dozen or so years ago, I would have felt his inclusion was justified. He was just that good and just that fun to watch.

But he did not retire about half a dozen years or so ago. In fact, entering the 2007 season he still has yet to retire. While I would normally not begrudge an athlete her or his chance to play her or his sport at the highest level for as long as possible, there also comes a time when things get ridiculous.

Normally, it is not that painful. When your normal, run-of-the-mill professional athlete is no longer able to play that athlete's chosen sport, then she or he is generally let go and is not picked up by anyone else. But that is rarely the case for the elite athlete. The elite athlete, if she or he is foolish enough to do so, can generally hang around for nearly forever. Eventually it just gets sad.

In the case of Brett Favre, it is not only sad it is grating and silly. Brett Favre, and the way that he has handled his career in the last five or six years, has turned his saga into one gigantic episode of Oprah.

It began, in one sense, with John Madden. It is no secret that Madden admires Favre's play. But he loves it to a point that is, quite simply, uncomfortable. He has gushed for years about Favre and his abilities. Yet, even more devastating for the sporting public, Madden began the trend of waxing (not particularly) eloquently about how much Favre "loves to play the game" and is "having fun out there."

Once Madden said it enough times, all of the dumbed down, irregular Madden facsimiles who do commentary for the NFL picked up on it and, consequently, every Packers game was contaminated with long soliloquies about how much fun Brett Favre is having playing the game of football. He has a big, ol' smile when he plays, we were told. Farve's idiotic jump-fake passes when he handed the ball off was further evidence his loving every minute of playing.

Somehow, through the unceasing repetition of this blather, the sporting world (or at least the sporting media) became captivated with Brett Favre's emotional state. As he got older and the years went by, the talk was always about whether or not Brett Favre was still having fun playing the game. When speculation about Favre possibly retiring grew in the passing years, the central question was not simply if he was going to come back or not, the question was about Favre's level of enjoyment. Does he still love the game? Is he still having fun out there? Is he still the happy, smiling gunslinger of yesteryear? The sports media became a bunch of amateur psychologists who acted as if Favre was a five-year-old at a birthday party. Do you think he is having fun? What would make him continue to love the game? Maybe he would come back to play for one more year if someone gave him another slice of cake or gave him a whack at the piñata.

Favre, for his part, has done nothing to squelch the ridiculous fawning over him. As the years have stretched on, so has the amount of time Favre has taken to decide whether or not he was going to return. Thus, the soap opera surrounding his situation has lingered more and more each off-season. And consequently Favre keeps turning Sportscenter into an episode of Dr. Phil (who, by the way, I hate with an absolutely unreasonable passion).

In the meantime, Favre's skills have continued to erode. The ol' gunslinger with the smile on his face is firing more blanks than bullets these days. That coupled with the fact that Favre's selfish comments and behavior in the last few off-seasons have actually been hurting the Packers, makes me mostly glad that he is coming back. As a Vikings fan I really cannot believe that it has reached a point where I can be glad of Favre's return to the Packers. Nonetheless, as long as an aging Favre is losing his skills and holding the Packers hostage, I hope he sticks around.

The one downfall, however, to Farve's return for future seasons is that the sporting public will continue to have to suffer through dumb sports reporters trying to clinically analyze Favre's state of mind. This massive group therapy session is both tedious and, at this point, useless. Favre is no longer what he once was and he has long since lost any unhateability factor.

I hate Brett Favre and I hate the Green Bay Packers.

THE TEAM I HATE THE MOST

Minnesota Vikings

The Original Whizzinator. Keep this in mind (although not too vividly) as we shall return to it.

Throughout the course of my life as a Vikings fan I have had to succumb to one simple truth: the team is dumb. I mean the whole team, top to bottom. All the way up from the highest levels of ownership on down to the locker room towel boys. They are all dumb.

This project has been a chronicle of the various ways that the Minnesota Vikings have made me hate every other team in the National Football League. But in reality, it has been more of an exercise in blaming the victim. The other teams in the league were, more or less, doing their job when they defeated or humiliated or embarrassed the Vikings. The critical component to each one of the sections in this book has been the Minnesota Vikings themselves. Were it not for the Purple I would not hate every team in the league.

Thus, the team I hate the most is the Vikings. For over a quarter of a century now I have watched their games and rooted for them and paid plenty of good money for tickets and merchandise. During that time they have won a few games and had a small measure of success. But the real defining characteristic of the team ever since I have been a fan has been a profound stupidity that has permeated every level of the organization. That, coupled with an ability to lose games (especially important games) in spectacular and heartbreaking fashion, has made the time I have spent following the club generally miserable. It is, by and large, not fun being a Vikings fan.

The team is hateable at every level. Their stupidity has never been the product of one bad apple, nor has it been sequestered within a short period of the franchise's history. This is the way that it has always been. With the exception of the few short months of the 1998 regular season, the team has been barely tolerable when it was winning and downright disgusting when it was losing. It is a situation that cannot be explained en masse, but rather needs further breakdown and elaboration. This is why I hate the various segments that make up the Minnesota Vikings:

<u>The Players</u>

Athletes are not exactly renown for their sparkling intelligence. But the Vikings seem to have employed an especially thick collection of human beings over the years. The latest, and perhaps most embarrassing, example was the infamous "love boat" scandal.

Some of the details of the whole incident are still a little murky. However, a certain amount is known, and that certain amount is kind of gross. In early October of 2005, members of the Vikings rented two boats to cruise Lake Minnetonka and to, let us say, socialize. The ridiculousness started before anyone got on the boat when someone in the neighborhood called the police to complain that certain folks who where in a limo stopped near the caller's property and urinated on the lawn.

Things only got worse. The alleged offending urinators were players headed to the boat party. After the two ships launched, there was allegedly lots of very open, very public, naughty conduct. It was also alleged that one player in particular arranged to have women of an extremely sociable nature flown in from Atlanta to make sure that everybody was enjoying themselves. Again, some of the details are murky (and frankly, I do not mind keeping them that way). And it has also been reported that not all of the players on the boats engaged in questionable behavior. But what is known is that members of the boat crew were not particularly happy with the conduct, felt threatened or in danger during the cruise, and were not overjoyed at having to clean up the remnants of the party. The three hour trip was cut short and four players were eventually charged in the incident. One player, Daunte Culpepper, was eventually cleared of all charges. The three other players, Fred Smoot, Bryant McKinnie, and Moe Williams, all pled guilty to minor charges.

It was a sad affair that immediately became the butt of jokes across the nation. The incident was so noteworthy that even late night talk show hosts took their shots at the team. Carolina Panther Steve Smith notably pretended to row a boat after he burned a mouthy Smoot (for the 483rd time that afternoon) for a touchdown in a subsequent game. People were selling t-shirts that mocked the cruise. And the local company that owned the boats has become a cultural touchstone in the twin cities.

Were this just a lone incident of bad behavior amongst Vikings players it might be brushed off as a relatively harmless error of judgment. After all, apparently everyone who participated in the naughty behavior was of a proper age and disposition and none of the boat crew was apparently scarred with anything more than disgusting memories. But it is not a lone incident. It is just the ickiest and most unusual in a long string of examples of the ridiculous actions of Vikings players.

There has also been the unfortunately typical string of domestic abuse and drunk driving arrests. These pointless and avoidable crimes are not just of recent vintage either. From about the mid-'80s to the early '90s it seemed like the team was not ready for a game unless a player had gotten arrested in the previous week. Apparently jail time helped them keep their edge.

More recent Vikings players have also found themselves doing time. There have been the same domestic abuse, drunk driving, and sexual abuse arrests. Yet, they have taken it up a notch. They have branched out to include whaling on other men and each other as well.

Of course, I would be remiss if I did not mention what was, prior to the love boat scandal, the most bizarre incident involving a Viking player's bad behavior. In the mid-'80s defensive lineman Keith Millard pled guilty to disorderly conduct. Apparently he was causing some trouble in a twin cities hotel. This, in and of itself, is, regrettably, not terribly uncommon. But what sent the situation (way) over the top was when Millard challenged the officers who reported to the scene to shoot at him because, as he stated, "my arms are more powerful than your guns."

Randy Moss also deserves a bit of mention again. Although some of his exploits have already been covered in previous sections, Moss does really stand out above the crowd. Randy actually does not fit the mold when it comes to the typical bad behavior of Vikings players. He (as far as it has ever been reported) never beat up a woman or ran his car into a telephone pole. And he was gone before the love boat set sail. Nor has Randy Moss ever struck me as being nearly as dumb as a great number of the Vikings players over the years.

Rather, Randy engaged in the sort of petulant behavior of a person who had rarely if ever been told "no" in his life. Most of Randy's bad behavior was much less malicious or criminal than it was silly and immature. He walked off of the field before a game was done. He bumped a traffic cop at a low speed. His car had marijuana in it. He claimed that he played, "when I want to play."

It was all just needlessly defiant, rebellious teenage antics. But they were never put to an end. Randy Moss did stupid things because he could. And nobody in the organization cared to take disciplinary actions. Things really escalated when Denny Green was fired and was replaced with Mike Tice. Which gets us to...

The Coaches

By this point in the project I think my feelings about the Mike Tice regime should be pretty clear. Thus, I shall only briefly reiterate what I have already expressed. Mike Tice began with the Vikings as an inexperienced and not terribly good head football coach. Mike Tice left the Vikings as an experienced and not terribly good head football coach.

The love boat scandal was the biggest disgrace of the 2005 season, but it was hardly the first. It became known prior to the 2005 campaign that Tice had been scalping his Super Bowl tickets for a large profit. There were also allegations that Tice aggressively campaigned players to use him as a conduit if they wanted to scalp their tickets. At first, Tice completely denied all of the allegations. However, less than a week later when it became clear that someone had enough information to call his bluff, he admitted to selling his tickets. He also tried to throw every other coach in the NFL under the bus by claiming that it was a league-wide practice. Eventually he was fined approximately one tenth of his salary for the 2005 season.

It was the greatest example of Tice's inability to handle the job or to learn from any of his previous mistakes. It should be no wonder then that Randy Moss spun out of control and that the love boat scandal happened under Tice's watch. If your team leader is engaged in this type of behavior (2005 was, mercifully, Tice's last season as head coach), then what else can you expect?

Tice's predecessor, Denny Green, was not nearly as incompetent or ridiculous. In fact, I have stated earlier in the project and I shall state again that I believe that Denny was somewhat unfairly vilified by Vikings fans and the local media. But as I have also stated earlier in this project, Denny brought a lot of it on himself with some of his own quotes and behavior. Ultimately, Denny Green made it difficult to defend him.

Denny often made statements that, given as much benefit of

the doubt as earthly possible, could only be rated as "not that bad." One such example occurred in the 1997 playoffs. The Vikings found themselves down by sixteen points at halftime to the New York Giants. The situation felt especially tenuous because for all of his regular season success to that point, Denny had yet to win a playoff game with the team. In fact, many speculated that a loss could cost Green his job.

Minnesota got a touchdown for the third quarter's lone score. Yet, as the clock kept ticking the situation got more and more desperate. With just a few minutes left in the game and with the team down by nine points, Denny inexplicably punted the ball instead of going for it on fourth down. Every Vikings fan in the world collectively screamed at their televisions when it happened. Luckily for Green the Giants blew up, including having a couple of defensive players fight with each other on the field, and the Vikings were able to muster ten points in the last ninety seconds of the game. It was a miraculous victory and the Vikings were extremely lucky to have won. Instead of acknowledging that fact, Green praised his own play calling, including the late punt. It was another typically miscalculated statement. Their likes were not rare during Denny's years as head coach.

Green's biggest foot-in-mouth moment actually happened in print. Denny published his autobiography, *No Room for Crybabies*, in late 1997. The publication would have been another unremarkable sports book were it not for the fact that Green threatened to sue the team's owners if they did not sell the team to Green. How Denny thought he would obtain the funds to purchase the franchise has been a source of speculation for years. Accordingly, the particularly juicy passages have continued to be fodder for the local sports media to this day. As good as a coach as Denny Green was, he was not what the kids like to call "media-savvy."

The other Vikings coaches of my lifetime have, in general, been slightly less embarrassing, although they had their moments. Les Steckel, of course, was a disaster from beginning to end. But

Jerry Burns was generally not too horrible, the occasional profanity-laced tirade aside. Bud Grant was and continues to be a local hero for his solid coaching and stoic manner. Bud's only inflammatory (and grossly inaccurate and stupid) comments came after his coaching career was finished when he advocated against Native American treaty rights.

So, with the exception of the unfortunate hiccup of the Les Steckel year, the Vikings coaches have been getting goofier ever since Bud. But there is one situation for which the Vikings have always seemed to be profoundly flawed and in constant flux. Which leads us to...

<u>Owners and Management</u>

The Vikings have done some unbelievably ridiculous things as it concerned personnel, trades, and the draft. The worst, of course, is the Herschel Walker trade. However, that ugly incident was covered in the Dallas Cowboys section. So, I will focus my concentration on some of the other examples of how the Vikings' stupidity is not the occasional slip-up but a serious trend.

There were, of course, the draft day blunders. In both 2002 and 2003 the Vikings were supposed to pick in the number seven slot. The shenanigans of 2002 began when Kansas City, who was picking just ahead of Minnesota, did not get its pick in on time. The Vikings had a window of opportunity to rush up to the podium and make their selection before Kansas City. Unfortunately the Vikings were not ready for such a possibility and missed the golden opportunity to make a pick one spot ahead of where they were supposed to make their selection. In 2003 the Vikings had just the opposite problem. Although they had the seventh pick, they did not actually choose a player until the ninth slot. The Vikings let their time expire and Jacksonville and Carolina jumped ahead of them. The team claimed that it still got the player it wanted at the nine spot (with Mike Tice attempting to quell a heavily booing crowd at the team's draft party by repeatedly asking them to "calm down"). Nonetheless, many were, and still are, convinced that the team did this on purpose because then-owner Red McCombs did not want to pay for a player at the higher draft slot.

Which gets us to Red McCombs. There was a point where the goofy Texas used car salesman was actually a hero in the twin cities. Red bought the team before the '98 season and coasted on the good feelings from that year. But it was all downhill from there. Red could not give an interview without clamoring for a new stadium or threatening to move the team. And he was legendarily cheap. He would use loopholes in the NFL salary cap rules to make sure he was spending enough money without getting anywhere near the salary ceiling. There were also stories of Red leaving the team's training facilities in various states of disrepair.

But the reason that he was briefly a hero was because he replaced the "gang of ten" who owned the team prior to him. This collection of imbeciles was defined by their inability to get along or to provide any direction or momentum for the team. It seemed like every week one member or collection of members would threaten to sue another member or collection of members. The Herschel Walker mess occurred under this ineffective regime, as did the brief Vikings career of Mossy Cade.

For those who do not know or do not remember, Cade was a defensive back who played for the Packers. His short career was dealt its most serious blow when he was convicted of a sex offence and did a stint of fifteen months in jail. When he was released, the Vikings immediately signed him to their squad. The public outcry was enough to make the team cut him about three minutes after they signed him. Nonetheless, he technically ended his NFL career as a Viking.

Of course, the "gang of ten" and Red McCombs had their problems, but at least they owned the team. The list of clowns who have claimed to want to buy the franchise is almost as long as the list of Vikings players that have been arrested. Some memorable crackpots include best-selling author Tom Clancy. The already pudgy Clancy showed up at a press conference in the late '90s in a huge, puffy Vikings jacket to announce his intentions to purchase the club. It turns out that the girth that Clancy showed at the press conference dwarfed the girth of his wallet and it became clear rather quickly that he was several hundreds of millions of dollars short of what would be necessary to buy the Vikings. Despite this shining example of unsustainable bravado another pretender would show up less than a decade later. When Red McCombs put the team up for sale, the first seemingly viable candidate was businessman Reggie Fowler. Quite a big deal was made about Fowler as he was poised to be the first African American owner of an NFL franchise. All of that hoopla would have been justified if Fowler actually had the money he claimed to have had. But he did not. In fact, he did not have a lot of things he claimed to have had, including the experience of playing in the Little League World Series. To his credit, Fowler did have enough cash to become a (no pun intended) minority owner of the team.

Thus, the ownership situation and personnel moves have often been a mess. The level of coaching has gotten increasingly embarrassing. And the players are generally an unlikable lot. Yet, the team continues to be, far and away, the most popular pro team in the twin cities. Why is that? For the answer we have to turn our attention to...

<u>The Fans</u>

Let us face facts. We have to lay some of the blame at our own feet. We keep supporting these slobs even though they break our hearts every year. We are just like a jilted lover who keeps letting an abusive partner back into the house and into our lives. We take the losses and the foolishness and we come back for more.

However, this is not to suggest that we are victims. The fact of the matter is that many of us are not that bright. For example, we were willing to make just as many excuses for Randy Moss as the team was willing to make for him. Having lived in the twin cities during Moss's entire tenure as a Viking and having listened to way too much sports talk radio, I know this to be true.

However, if you want some slightly more empirical evidence, I will refer you to a poll done by the Star Tribune newspaper around the start of the 1993 season. The poll question asked who the fans thought should be the starting quarterback for the team that year. Admittedly, the supposed front runners of Sean Salisbury and Jim McMahon were hardly the cream of the crop. Nonetheless, the choice of Vikings fans was Gino Toretta. This choice was based on the strength of a couple of decent preseason games. Toretta, while on the Vikings roster that year, did not attempt a pass for the team. In fact, the only five completions of his NFL career happened in the 1996 season over the span of two games for Seattle. Toretta spread those five completions over sixteen attempts and experienced one touchdown and one interception each.

Picking Gino Toretta to be the starter for your favorite NFL franchise is dumb. Thus, it falls in line with the rest of the franchise from top to bottom. Vikings fans (myself very much included) are just as much culprits as we are victims.

All of which brings us back to the Original Whizzinator. The O.W. is, of course, a plastic device that is in the shape of a part of a man's anatomy and is meant to help men beat drug tests.

It is also something that caused further embarrassment for the Vikings. The 2005 season was so comically humiliating for the team that the O.W. had to have happened that year. Running back Onterrio Smith was detained in an airport when a security guard discovered a dry powder among his personal effects. At first, the powder was believed to be an illegal drug of some sort, but it turned out to be dried urine. The powder, mixed with water, was to go into the O.W. and was to be stealthily distributed during a drug test. Smith, who had a history of drug problems and suspensions claimed that the O.W. belonged to his cousin. Regardless, the story was leaked and Smith, who missed a drug test in the wake of the O.W. incident, was kicked out of the league for that year. He has not played in the NFL since.

The O.W. is also the perfect symbol for the franchise. It often seems like the team is not real, but rather an inadequate facsimile of an NFL franchise. They also, as illustrated in Smith's case, create more problems than they solve. And, in the long run, they do not work and are cause for ridicule. The Minnesota Vikings are the Original Whizzinator of the NFL and I hate them for it.

Hate is such a strong word. Which is why it was the appropriate word to define this project. I really cannot stand that I keep watching this team. I know how the story ends. I have seen it nearly thirty times now. It never changes. It never gets better. In fact, it only gets worse.

And yet, I keep coming back. Every fall I get excited again and I can hardly wait for that first kickoff, even though I once saw it run back for a touchdown which led to the lone victory for a 1-15 team. I start talking about the team's prospects and I start reading all of the prognostications on the season. And when that first game finally arrives, I watch. I am either sitting in a stadium seat or in front of the television, hoping that this is finally the year.

It never is. It never has been and I am fairly well convinced that it never will be. It is just a repackaged version of the same old kick in the pants. Despite knowing that, each year I turn around, bend over, and take that swift boot to my bottom as if I was ignorant of its inevitable arrival.

The worst part is that I do it gladly. The interminably long off-season is just enough time to forgive and forget (although who truly ever forgets?). And then it is the same routine. The Vikings find a novel way to lose and be embarrassing and I swear them off forever. Until fall rolls around.

I hate the Minnesota Vikings. I really hate them with all of my heart and soul.

I hate them because I love them.

Printed in the United States
96372LV00003B/5/A

9 781934 248522